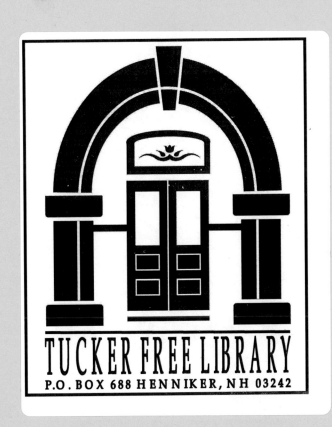

Jennifer's Way
KITCHEN

Jennifer's Way KITCHEN

**Easy Allergen-Free,
Anti-Inflammatory Recipes
for a Delicious Life**

JENNIFER ESPOSITO

with Eve Adamson

GLUTEN-FREE, GRAIN-FREE, DAIRY-FREE, EGG-FREE, SOY-FREE,
CORN-FREE, REFINED-SUGAR-FREE RECIPES FROM
THE OWNER OF THE BELOVED JENNIFER'S WAY BAKERY

GRAND CENTRAL
Life&Style
NEW YORK • BOSTON

MY FIRST BOOK, Jennifer's Way, *was dedicated to all the celiacs, diagnosed and undiagnosed. I feel for anyone who must walk down the scary road that this disease can be. I dedicate this book to all of them again, but not to just them. This book is for everyone who deals with health questions that go unanswered and health issues that go undiagnosed. I believe times are changing and that people are realizing the latest pill is not the answer. While there is a time and a place for medication, it is my belief that what we eat can dramatically impact how we feel. I am not just a believer in this. I live it, and practice what I preach every day, and this is why I dedicate this book to all those people who are doing the same, or want and need to begin that process.*

I can be changed by what happens to me.
But I refuse to be reduced by it.

—MAYA ANGELOU

Come in

We're

OPEN

Did Yo

PLEAS
YOUR FEEDBACK

All Baking
Premis

CONTENTS

How It All Began

It all started with a chocolate chip cookie. Warm, ooey-gooey, and sweet—chocolaty chunks inside a soft, tender cookie with the perfect crunchy exterior. I baked them every year at Christmastime, and what a treat they were! I remember that chocolate-chip-cookie aroma seeping into every room in the house. I remember eating them just after they came out of the oven. But most of all, I remember the thrill of making them with my sister. That's what really made those simple chocolate chip cookies so special. It was tradition. It was comfort. Baking them made me feel happy and connected. It completed the holidays for me.

Ever since I was a kid, food has been a huge part of my life. Birthday parties with friends and family meant homemade chocolate cake. Saturday mornings meant fresh-made pancakes and French toast covered in butter and real maple syrup. Sunday Italian dinners started at three in the afternoon and went on for hours. For me, the love of food, and especially of sharing food with the people I love, was one of the most important aspects of growing up.

As an adult, my world suddenly tilted. After 20 years of unanswered health questions and misdiagnoses (you can read more about that in my first book, *Jennifer's Way*), I was diagnosed with a devastating case of celiac disease. I learned that the thing I loved with such a passion was also the cause of my illness. Food was my enemy. How could this be? How could something I loved so dearly, something that gave me life and so much happiness, be killing me slowly?

I felt betrayed. I was a mess (to say the very least)—forced to face a new, uncertain future where food was suddenly safe or not safe, where restrictions and limits dictated every choice I made. When fear seeps in, baking cookies isn't an easy option anymore, and that left a hole in my life. I knew I needed to give myself time to heal, learn, and grow. I came to terms with what my diagnosis would mean and slowly learned to change my lifestyle to rebuild my health. While food could certainly hurt me, I learned that it could also be lifesaving. Soul-saving too.

But it would take some time to get to that place. At first, I struggled to understand all the things I could no longer eat. Gluten, which I was told at diagnosis I could never eat again, I understood. I was already mourning all the things I could no longer enjoy—bread and bagels, pizza and pasta, cake and those dearly beloved chocolate chip cookies. But I gradually began to discover that in my case (and for many others with autoimmune or other chronic conditions), what I couldn't eat went far beyond gluten. I also reacted negatively to dairy products, eggs, soy, and refined sugar. This was a long learning process, as I kept discovering more and more foods I couldn't eat without worsening my symptoms. The more items I had to cross of my "Okay" list, the more my food landscape seemed barren and depressing. In my lowest moments I was so ill that it was difficult to summon the energy or optimism to do anything about it. I became severely malnourished, but I didn't know how to fix it safely. I used what little energy I had to search for answers about how to heal myself and also get the essential vitamins and minerals I needed.

I knew my mourning was about more than the laundry list of foods I'd cut out of my life. I needed to find some kind of peace and joy with food again, because if I couldn't find that, eating hardly seemed worth the effort. For me, losing the joy was even worse than losing any particular food I loved. Sure, I missed bagels, but even more I missed the sense of community and belonging that food had always contributed to my life.

> I needed to find some kind of **peace and joy** with food again, because if I couldn't find that, eating hardly seemed worth the effort.

Where was the joy? I certainly wasn't finding it at the supermarket. The "gluten-free" foods most stores had to offer were filled with empty calories, preservatives, loads of sodium, and tons of sugar, not to mention the blatant presence of other allergens I could no longer eat. These processed "health foods" had no redeeming qualities, especially not good taste. To me, they tasted like cardboard, or a damp sponge.

I longed for that joy, along with a way to heal myself. Was it too much to ask to have both in my life? Finally, as with so many other things in life, I realized that if what I wanted didn't exist, I was going to have to create it myself. I was going to have to get back in the kitchen, where I had started all those years before, making those chocolate chip cookies in the fullness of food freedom. This too would be a long learning process, and I would make many mistakes, but I would learn by trial and error how to cook and bake for my life now—for my new normal. No matter how difficult, I was determined to get there. I wanted to find my food freedom again.

I began with simple meals that were naturally gluten free, with lean proteins and tons of vegetables; fish with more vegetables, or vegetables and beans. Surely vegetables would heal me if gluten was hurting me, right? Wrong. Even on this supposedly pure diet, I still felt ill—not to mention uninspired. So, I thought, maybe I would enjoy baking more than day after day of steaming endless greens. I began to experiment with gluten-free baking, which is a real challenge. I made many failed cakes, cookies, breads, and what were supposed to be muffins. But I kept trying, kept experimenting, kept changing the formula, and finally, finally I discovered some tricks that really worked.

I began to bake foods that tasted good and, even better, foods that were also nutritionally rich. I baked cakes and breads and muffins that were delicious. I was in heaven! But then I began to feel even more ill, and I realized that all I was eating were my baked goods. They didn't contain gluten, or any of the other allergens I could no longer eat, but one cannot live on gluten-free bread alone. There had to be a middle ground, or a way in, to a lifestyle that was both satisfying and deeply nutritious.

There had to be a **middle ground**, or a way in, to a lifestyle that was both satisfying and deeply nutritious.

At that point, I realized I needed to go back to the drawing board and get to know the true underlying issue: my gut. It became extremely clear to me that my gut was "angry" with every food choice I made, and I knew I needed some professional advice to help heal it. I began working closely with my doctor, who also has celiac disease, so he understood exactly what I was going through. He explained to me that I had a leaky gut and what that meant for my body and diet. Damage to my digestive tract had created small tears in the lining, and these tears were allowing food particles to get into my bloodstream before they were digested. The problem was causing my immune system to overreact. Healing my gut would keep the food where it belonged and calm the overzealous immune response.

I went on a quest for more information. I read everything I could and made myself a guinea pig in my quest to heal. I took L-glutamine, which is good for healing the gut lining, and herbs that my doctor mixed up for me. I also began to pay very close attention to the state of my gut—how I felt when I ate or didn't eat, and how I felt when I ate different things. I started to realize that the gut is more important than I could have imagined. As my doctor always says (I'm pretty sure Hippocrates said it first), "The root of all disease begins in the gut."

I learned a lot more, once I really started paying attention to both the quiet and loaded messages my gut was sending me daily: mood changes, brain fog, exhaustion, even hair falling out. I learned that my mood in particular was directly connected to the state of my gut. When my stomach didn't feel well, I felt more down and depressed. I realized that I developed pain in my chest and tightness in my throat when I ate vegetables, especially raw. My gut wasn't sufficiently healed to digest all that fiber, and I had a particular problem with beans. All of those safe, gluten-free veggies had been working against me the whole time.

I also realized the importance of the quality of my food. I started paying attention to where my food came from, how it was grown, and whether or not it was organic. The cleaner and purer my food source, the better I began to feel. Slowly, after much time and patience, my gut began to stabilize. I still had flares, but overall, I felt better. I began to enjoy food again, at a deeper level, because the food I ate that tasted so good was also repairing my health rather than hurting me.

After many years of stockpiling information, concocting messes and successes in the kitchen, and nurturing a happier gut, I began blogging at JennifersWay.org, which has now turned into LivingFreeJennifer.com, about my experience with this tricky disease. I wanted to share all the information I had uncovered with anyone who might want to listen. Up until this point, the people in the celiac community I'd tapped into were my only allies—they truly understood this journey I was on. I wanted my blog to give back to a community that had helped me so much. It soon became a one-stop shop, not only for information about celiac disease but also for my favorite recipes and food advice. I also quickly became a celiac advocate, speaking out about what this disease really means for the people living, struggling, and thriving with it. Being in the public eye helped me expand my mission and reach beyond my small corner of the Internet. The blog opened a new path to connect, through emails, texts, and tweets, to people from all around the world. Readers need answers and help. They want to know what they can do for their health on a daily basis, beyond what their doctors have told them. I wanted, and needed, to find a way to respond to everyone else out there just like me.

My answer was to collect everything I'd learned into a book, *Jennifer's Way: My Journey with Celiac Disease—What Doctors Don't Tell You and How You Can Learn to Live Again*. And I didn't stop there—I opened my tiny bakery, Jennifer's Way, on East 10th Street in New York City, which continues to be a safe haven for anyone dealing with gluten and allergy issues. I brought all my favorite and most beloved recipes into that bakery and I baked and baked: bagels, breads, cupcakes, cookies, and an assortment of other delights. I saw firsthand that it wasn't just about the bagel or a safe treat. It is about giving people a piece of their lives back. Being able to celebrate a birthday with an actual *cake* again, or just enjoying a cookie without worry, means so much more than just giving someone some food to eat. It is giving someone freedom.

The response from people wanting clean, safe, delicious food has been overwhelming. And it wasn't only from other celiacs and people who suffered with autoimmune diseases—it was also from moms who would come by looking for school-safe snacks for their children to share with friends. It was from people struggling with other health issues, and it was also from people who are healthy, but want to stay that way. It was from the savvy shoppers and foodies who knew that they wanted only the best ingredients in their food. It was from people who just know a damn good cookie when they eat one. It was coming from all directions. I soon realized that people wanted my products who couldn't come to my bakery, and so I began shipping them. It's a big job, but it is my pleasure and my life's mission.

But there is more to my mission than baking cookies. I realized there was still something missing. People continue to ask me the same two questions: *But how do*

People continue to ask me the same two questions: *But how do you live?* and *What do you eat every day?*

you live? and *What do you eat every day?* I get these two questions more than any others, not just from people with celiac disease but from those with other autoimmune diseases, as well as those who just feel better when they eat cleaner. That's when I conceived this book.

This book is a guide for anyone who wants to reclaim health. In it, I tell you what I do and how I eat, but it is also much more than what I do in my day-to-day to stay on top of my health. This is a book about eliminating the true villain that lurks within us all: *inflammation.* Throughout my journey knowingly living with celiac disease for the past eight years, this is the one problem that always resurfaces. It is a problem not just for those dealing with autoimmune diseases, but for many other chronic health issues. It's a nasty word, inflammation, and it causes disease in anyone. That's why I made this book a guide to everything I do and make and eat to keep inflammation down and stay healthy, while still enjoying the wonderful flavors of the foods I love. By no means is eating to combat inflammation boring or unflavorful. I couldn't do it if that were the case because the pleasure of food is one of the biggest joys in life.

This book is a cookbook, but it is different than most cookbooks. Not only does every recipe have major anti-inflammatory components, but all recipes are also completely free of gluten, dairy, soy, eggs, corn, and refined sugars (the foods that are most likely to be problems for many people). The recipes are organized around three key modes:

1.   **PURE Recipes for Healing:** This covers what to eat to help the body decrease inflammation and allow the immune system and gut to rest. I read a wonderful book that said (I'm paraphrasing): The gut is the queen of the castle and if she is upset, she will take down the kingdom. This couldn't be more correct. This is why anyone and everyone can benefit from eating Pure. Yes, it's especially helpful for those dealing with autoimmune issues, but it is also for all who want to allow the body to do some healing. In times of inflammation, this is the chapter to live in. You will find recipes like gut-healing Bone Broth (page 73), soups, mashes, gentle dishes of meat or fish with cooked vegetables, and healing tonics.

    Honestly, this is how I eat most of the time. For me, I find it truly helps with the constant inflammation that comes from having an autoimmune disease. Maybe you will want to live here too. It's more restrictive, but it feels so good when your inflammation subsides, so for me it is more than worthwhile.

    The Pure recipes contain no grains at all. They also don't contain nuts, seeds, nightshade vegetables (tomatoes, peppers, eggplants, or potatoes), or raw vegetables, which can be difficult to digest. I also recommend staying away from coffee, alcohol, and other stimulants when you are eating Pure.

2. **CLEAN Recipes for Living:** When you feel good and inflammation is down, this section covers what to eat on a daily basis to maintain your health. The recipes are all clean, allergen free, and nourishing, but they reintroduce some things you were not eating when you were eating Pure—things a healed gut can manage now and then, like some gluten-free grains, small amounts of nuts and seeds, and nightshade vegetables, to name a few. You can also try some raw vegetables (like salads), and you can add coffee back if you really want it; just stick to organic coffee. But I'd also try to drink green tea too, just for its anti-inflammatory benefits. If you want to add back alcohol, look for types without gluten (of course) and with the least possible sugar, and keep it to a minimum.

3. **INDULGENT Recipes for Splurging (in Moderation):** These are my kick-your-heels-up, play-like-a-kid recipes. In this section, you'll add a little more natural sweetener to some of the recipes, and you will also find recipes that are a little richer, but still nutrient dense, nourishing, and delicious. These recipes are for enjoying once in a while. From Fauxstess Cupcakes (like the version you ate when you were a kid, but safe—see page 273), to Roasted Butternut Squash Lasagna (page 251) and Jennifer's Famous BBQ Baby Back Ribs (page 249), every recipe is still clean...just a little bit more decadent.

Best of all, I created every single one of these recipes with joy. I strive to recapture the deliciousness of those free-eating days in *every* section of this book, without ever compromising your gut health or food sensitivities. Are you feeling inflamed or bloated or overly tired but you still want dessert? I've got just the thing for you. Are you feeling great and want to celebrate a special occasion? I provide exactly what you crave. Are you bored of the same old things every day, and just want to spice up your normal menu? I will help you expand your culinary boundaries without sacrificing your health or launching you into a week of down days. I don't want to focus on everything you can't have. This cookbook is about all the glorious, amazing, delectable, nutrient-rich foods you can enjoy and will get to enjoy every single day, and still keep that inflammation at bay. I have never believed in depriving myself of anything I crave, and that is how most of these recipes were conceived. I just wasn't willing to eat foods that weren't fun and delicious—crunchy, tasty, yummy, savory, ooey-gooey. It's the only way I want to eat, for the rest of my life.

The book begins with advice on ingredient quality, how to keep an allergen-free and inflammation-free kitchen, and the tools and equipment that can make cooking easier for you. I've also sprinkled some thoughts and advice on some of the therapies and lifestyle interventions I use throughout the book.

Then, the recipes. But I didn't want them to be organized like every other cookbook, by meals or ingredients. Instead, I organized the recipes according to how I eat, why, and in what order. Living with an autoimmune disease means your body is in a constant state of defense against internal attack, and that's why it's so important to keep inflammation down and eat nutrient-dense foods. This is how you stay on top of your life, in every way, even if you don't have an autoimmune disease. Because we all know that on some days, we feel okay, and on other days, we don't. On some days, we can get through the day as long as we are fueled with clean, nutrient-dense foods, and on other days, we aren't feeling so well and need to nurture the gut a little more carefully. And then there are those days when we feel strong and good and want a treat.

I didn't organize these recipes by meals because I also never want to tell you what you should eat for breakfast, lunch, or dinner. So I've organized the recipes by type of food, such as breads, soups, mashes, smoothies, or sweet things. If you're like me, you might have soup for breakfast, mashed butternut squash for lunch, and a smoothie for dinner, and I want you to feel that you can do that here.

This is how I live. This is what I know. If you want to enjoy delicious food but still eat clean, quench the fire of inflammation, be strong, nurture your gut, boost your immunity, and take control of your health in ways you might not have been able to do before, come join me at the table. Your days of deprivation and believing you can no longer eat food that is both delicious and safe for you are over. This is your guide and your safe haven, and everything between these two covers is guaranteed to keep you living safe, pure, clean, indulgent...and free.

> Your days of deprivation and believing you can no longer eat food that is both **delicious** and **safe for you** are over.

Welcome to My World

If you are reading this book, I'm guessing we have a lot in common. I love life and all it brings, but I especially love the food. I love making it and sharing it. I love the joy it brings to people. Food didn't always bring me joy, though. For too many years, I struggled with my undiagnosed chronic illness, celiac disease, and food became the enemy.

Living with chronic disease isn't so different from regular life, but it is much more difficult. Every bite you take, every hour of sleep missed, every stressful toxic environment you're in, every pill you take or supplement you choose—all can have a dramatic effect on your long- and short-term health and happiness. This is true for everyone, but it is amplified for those with a chronic illness.

Who wants to live that way, having to be so careful all the time? For me it was not an option, and that has made all the difference. I'm not saying that I don't have hard days, because I do; but I have found foods, rituals, eliminations, and a new way to look at my situation. Since my last book, I have been asked by so many who read it, "Now what? How do I LIVE?" Well, I've been stockpiling these recipes and life tips to share with you ever since the first person asked me that question, and I promise I have some great tools for all who want to take back control of their health. In doing this, you must take a good look at not only your food, but *all* the inflammatory triggers in your life. If you don't, a clean, healthy diet will be rendered useless. Yes, *useless*.

Okay, let's get started. First, here are the top two major things in life that I've found kick that nasty inflammation into high gear for all of us: stress and toxins. Here's what I do about them.

Stress   Stress is the number-one most potent way to inflame not just your body but also your heart, mind, and soul, and it is the one that gives me the most trouble. I will be honest. I am still trying to win this battle. I am a work-in-progress, as we all are. Life is hard and stress is a part of it. This is something I've had to come to terms with: Sometimes, things happen to you in your life that are not happy or pleasant. Sometimes, things happen that are downright brutal. When things like this happen to me—like a diagnosis of celiac disease, to name just one of many things that have happened to me—it can leave me in a hole. To get out of that hole, I've learned to look for the lesson and consider every experience, good or bad, as a learning opportunity for growth. For example, if I had never been diagnosed with celiac disease, I wouldn't be writing this book, and I wouldn't have as my life's purpose helping people from around the world who struggle with health issues. That has meant more to me than pretty much anything else in my life (other than my pups).

But finding the lesson isn't always easy in the moment. Here are some things I do to help me climb out of the hole and get through the immediate real-time stress:

- **ACCEPTANCE.** Life happens, and then you grow. You can waste a lot of energy wanting something not to be the way it is, but that won't change anything. There are always things you can change (especially the way you think about something), but accepting reality instead of living in denial can make a huge difference in how much stress you feel about a certain situation. Take a diagnosis, for example (although this works for anything). You can wish you didn't have a chronic health issue. You can be angry about it. You can try to blame someone or something. You can get depressed about it, or get anxiety about it, or just be generally pissed off that your life has taken a turn for the worse. You can lose hope and see no future for yourself. Or you can accept your situation, take a deep breath, and decide that this is now part of your reality, and that's okay. Only then can you finally move forward with your life and start working on finding your new normal.

- **SELF-CARE AND KINDNESS.** It's easy to be hard on yourself. So many of us do this. You say negative things to yourself. You deprive yourself. You make yourself suffer. None of that does any good. When you are having health issues, or emotional issues, or both, what you really need is self-care. You are hurting, and you don't need to make it worse on yourself. Give yourself a break. Think positive things about yourself, and say positive things to yourself. It may seem difficult at first, but it's a habit to be negative, and it's a habit to be kind to yourself. The more you do it, the easier it gets.

- **MEDITATION.** Along this windy, curvy road called life, I can't always see what's around the next corner. When I get to it, I don't always like what is there. To deal with the stress that comes with living life this way, I have found that meditation really helps. For years, people told me I should meditate, but I never thought it was for me. Then I hit a really crazy, hard time many years ago (this was before I was diagnosed), and I began searching everywhere for some peace. Finally, I decided to give meditation a try, and it became the single best thing I could do for myself. Meditation is self-care at its most powerful. In order to give both your body and mind a rest, you need to be able to find true silence, and that's what meditation does. If you are like me, working even when you are sleeping, constantly busy in body and mind (making plans, writing recipes, singing songs, my mind always moving), meditation is the only time when I can really get silent and allow body and mind to just be.

  I suggest starting slow and following just one rule: Be kind to yourself.

  So how do you do it? I suggest starting slow and following just one rule: Be kind to yourself. You don't have be perfect or get it "right." There is no "right." Just sit quietly, close your eyes, and pay attention to your breath. Breathe in through your nose for five seconds, hold your breath for five seconds, and exhale for five seconds. While you do this, if thoughts come into your mind, gently say to yourself, "Now now." Sometimes I like to repeat three words to myself, over and over, like a mantra: "Peace, love, light." Eventually, I can feel my body and mind start to release.

  You could also listen to guided meditations. Personally, I love doing this and there are hundreds of them out there. Deepak Chopra has some amazing meditations you can download that have helped me tremendously.

  The more you do this, the easier it gets and the more you will crave it. Please try it. It is the single best thing you can do for your health, your happiness, and your life.

- **GRATITUDE.** When you are feeling stressed or low, you probably aren't thinking about all the things that you are grateful for, but by the same token, if you think about all the things you are grateful for, it's hard to feel stressed or low. There were days when my autoimmune disease had me on my knees, work was driving me crazy, and life just seemed tougher than it was the day before. During these times, I go down that hole again, and that's when I start making the wrong food decisions and getting off track with my sleep. It's a downward spiral, and when I realize I am doing it, that's when I purposefully switch into gratitude mode.

  Some people will tell you to keep a gratitude journal, but I've never been good at that. If that's not you, do what I do and just stop what you are doing for a moment and consciously acknowledge one thing you are grateful for.

I remember one day when I was walking to work. I was exhausted, in a bad mood, inflamed, hormonal, and hungry. Yuck. Then I looked up and saw the clouds for the first time that day. It was 3 p.m., and I had not looked at the sky or even noticed the day *at all*. I had been too plugged in to my own nonsense. When I looked up, not only did I notice that the sky was a beautiful blue, but that there were little soft, fluffy clouds floating slowly by. In that moment, I was suddenly so grateful for those happy clouds. I focused all my attention on them. I was so grateful I noticed them. And just like that, my day changed. The power of gratitude really is incredible.

> The power of gratitude really is incredible.

Another way I practice gratitude is by sitting with my furry friends. Pets make a huge impact on stress levels. My best friend in life was my golden retriever, Frankie, who has now passed away. When he was getting old, I would deliberately stop and sit with him and pet him and really feel his fur under my hand. I was so grateful for those moments, as I reminded myself that I wouldn't always be able to do that. I was, and still am, so grateful for his love and friendship.

But you don't need to have a pet to feel grateful. Any time you can feel it, do it. It will keep stress and therefore inflammation at bay, and increase those feel-good endorphins that make you happy and therefore healthy.

Toxins

If you live with toxic chemicals in your home due to cleaning products like harmful soaps and deodorizers, if you live with toxic mold, or if you put toxic chemicals in your body through skin absorption directly into your system, you cannot fully conquer inflammation. Have you ever looked at what's in your cleaning products? Have you considered what residue remains on your dishes and kitchen surfaces? What about your clothes and skin? What chemicals do you use to wash your clothes, or clean your bathtub?

It's impossible to eliminate all chemical exposure, but you can definitely reduce it significantly in your home. There is no need to use toxic chemicals to clean anything in your home, not to mention take care of your skin and hair. There are many wonderful natural products out there that work just as well. Here are some ideas:

- **MAKE YOUR OWN CLEANER:** Combine 1 cup apple cider vinegar with 5 cups water and put it in a spray bottle. This is all you need to clean your counters, bathroom, and even your floors. I also use tea tree oil as a homemade cleaner, because it kills mold and makes things smell clean and fresh. Put five drops in a bottle with 2½ cups water and spray on anything you want to deodorize or de-mold.

- **REPLACE YOUR PERSONAL HYGIENE PRODUCTS.** What's in your face cream, body lotion, deodorant, toothpaste, and makeup? Most likely, toxic chemicals. None of that is necessary. Look for natural, clean brands that won't increase your toxic burden. I know it sounds simple, but I seriously use coconut oil for just about everything. I use it to take off my makeup, as a skin moisturizer, even to deep-clean my gums by taking a tablespoonful of coconut oil each morning, before I do anything else, and swishing it around in my mouth for ten minutes. This is called "pulling" and it cleans toxic bacteria out of the mouth. It also feels great, after you get over the gag factor. (It gets better fast, trust me.)

  I also make sure my deodorant doesn't contain any aluminum, which can be absorbed through the skin and can be dangerous for the body, especially for those with autoimmune issues.

  I use Tom's of Maine toothpaste, which is a natural brand. And, sorry if it's TMI, but I don't use tampons anymore. Believe it or not, I use pads because I think we must allow the body to do what it needs to do. Let it take in what it needs and let go of what it doesn't without interference.

  As far as beauty products and makeup, there are some gluten-free brands. One I like is Afterglow. However, do your homework here, as formulas constantly change and the market for natural beauty products is growing rapidly. There are many choices out there, so I recommend trying out different kinds to find what works for your skin and your personality.

- **DETOXIFY YOUR BEAUTY ROUTINE:** Here are three recipes for beauty detoxifying that I use frequently: two bath soaks and a face mask.

detox bath soak

½ cup baking soda
Handful Epsom salt
2 tablespoons apple cider vinegar
Any essential oil you enjoy (optional)

Add all the ingredients to a hot bath as the water runs. Soak for up to 20 minutes, whenever you feel toxic or just need to calm down. Daily is fine, but I probably do this about once a week. Rinse with a cool shower to help rinse away the toxins you just sweat out.

coconut bath time

½ cup coconut oil
1 cup Epsom salt
A few drops lavender oil

Add all the ingredients to a hot bath as the water runs. Soak for up to 20 minutes. Rinse with a cool shower to help rinse away the toxins you just sweat out.

life is never dull facial mask

Makes 1 mask

2 tablespoons organic cocoa powder
2 tablespoons ground espresso
½ teaspoon ground cinnamon
2 tablespoons coconut oil
1 teaspoon raw honey

In a small bowl, combine the cocoa, espresso, and cinnamon. Add the coconut oil and honey and combine to form a paste. Apply the mask to the face and let dry. Leave on for up to 20 minutes.

To remove, wet a washcloth with warm water and place on your face to break up the mask. Splash water on your face until the mask is gone. Store any unused mask in the refrigerator for up to a few days.

I tell you all of this because I want you to keep the big picture in mind, but, of course, what most people ask me about is what I eat, what they should eat, and how to fit cooking and nutrient-dense, delicious eating into their lives so they can find a new normal that feels just as good as the old normal. In that spirit, let's get back to the main subject of this book: glorious, pure, clean, indulgent, delicious *food!*

Cleaning Up Your Kitchen

First things first: Let's get your kitchen safe and ready for cooking! Before you start filling up your refrigerator and pantry with precious, fresh, naturally clean food, you need to get your house in order. This requires a hard look at your living situation and how you and your family function around food. Do you live alone or with a partner? Do you have children or roommates who don't need to be gluten free? How much control do you have over the food in your home and the places it's stored, prepared, and cooked?

If you live alone or are otherwise in charge of your family's food, *you* get to control the rules because you are probably the one doing the shopping and cooking. But communication is key—it's not just setting rules, but explaining them fully to the people you live with you so that keeping a safe kitchen becomes a team effort. Everyone in the household needs to understand why you are doing this and how important it is. If you find yourself not fully in charge of your space, you may need to stand up for your needs—your very life could depend on it! A clean kitchen truly is the foundation for regaining your food freedom. These are the ground rules I recommend with great seriousness:

1. **GO GLUTEN FREE, HOUSEHOLD-WIDE.** It may sound drastic, but if it is at all possible, the entire household should go gluten free, whether it is medically required for everyone or not. Those who don't have a problem with gluten and want it can get their gluten on the outside. It may be easier than you think to get everyone on board. You'll get to participate fully in family meals because they will be safe for you, and you can help keep your family healthy by eating clean foods from the earth that just happen to be naturally gluten free. Household members can also help you stick to your plan by not waving

25

temptation in your face, as it can be difficult to go cold turkey at first. (I can tell you this, however: Once you feel how much better things get when you get gluten completely out of your life, and then get "glutened" a few times and have a relapse, you will have a very strong motivation to avoid the stuff.)

2. **DO A CLEAN SWEEP.** Go through every cabinet, shelf, and drawer and rid yourself of *all* the boxed or packaged "food" that contains a long list of ingredients. If it's processed, trash it, gluten or no gluten. Keep an eye out for the few exceptions—very simple foods like brown rice or quinoa, for example, may come in boxes or packages, but in most cases, the ingredient lists will be just one or two items long. My rule is: If you want to eat something out of a box, first look at the ingredient list and count. How many ingredients are there? If there are more than four or five, I would toss it. Can you read and pronounce *all* the ingredients, or do they look like chemical additives and artificial things? If the latter, toss it. And do you know what each ingredient is? If you see items that you cannot pronounce and you aren't sure what they are (even things like "natural flavors," if they don't specify what they contain), I recommend the trash can as the best place for them.

3. **IF IT'S MOSTLY SUGAR OR STARCH, TOSS IT.** Refined sugar, or even unrefined sugar (like raw sugar, raw honey, and pure maple syrup), is bad for your gut in large amounts. A little natural sugar can make life a joy, but the refined stuff is pure poison. If sugar is the first ingredient in any food item, even if it seems "natural" or is labeled "gluten free," put it down and back away.

4. **CLEAN UP YOUR HARDWARE.** After you have gotten rid of what's hiding in your cabinets, pantry, refrigerator, and freezer, it's time to look at your appliances, dishes, and anything that touches the food you eat. If you live alone, it's easy to thoroughly clean your appliances (although toasters are hard—you may want to get a new one), cookware, and serving ware, not to mention dish rags and kitchen towels, and keep everything totally free of cross-contamination. (Also look out for gluten crumbs in your condiments!) If you live in a house where gluten also lives (although see the first item on this list), then it is absolutely crucial that you have a separate, totally pure, gluten-free-upon-pain-of-death toaster, pots and pans, dishes, and utensils. I'm not kidding. Just keep them separate, and ask that all gluten-containing products and appliances be kept clearly separate and preferably covered.

   You can make this fun—try picking out dishware or utensils in a different color that stands out and makes you happy, and makes it easy for everyone to distinguish what's yours. Label if necessary: GLUTEN FREE ONLY! If you have children who must

FOOD LABEL FACT: ORDER MATTERS

Food labels can be informative, but they can also be deceiving. You just have to know what to look for. It's useful to know that ingredients are listed in order of how much the food contains. For example, if sugar is listed first, that food has more sugar than anything else.

be gluten free, different colors and large labels make it easier for them to quickly identify which items are for them. (But again, if you have children, *see item #1 on this list!*)

While it may seem like an investment to spring for separate gluten-free dishes, utensils, cookware, and appliances (like your own special gluten-free toaster or toaster oven), this is particularly important...*crucial*...if you or anyone in your family has celiac disease. Remember, just one-third of a teaspoon of gluten will harm or kill the villi in your small intestine and make you ill. Cross-contamination is a huge issue and one to take seriously, both for you and other household members. Again, communication is key here. People you live with and/or interact frequently with (such as at work) need to understand that this is not just a whim of yours. It is a serious health requirement.

> Cross-contamination is a **huge issue** and one to **take seriously,** for both you and other household members.

SUGAR AND STARCH STEALTH

Sugar comes in many guises. If an ingredient list says "sugar," that's pretty self-explanatory. Unless you live in a cave, you probably also know that high-fructose corn syrup is a highly processed sweetener that the health-conscious want to avoid. However, refined sugar comes under many other names that aren't so obvious. If you see any of these on a food label (or longer names that include these words), avoid! (Note that they often end in "-ose" or "-ol.")

Carbitol

Corn sweetener/ corn syrup

Dextrose

Diglycerides

Disaccharides

Fructooligo- saccharides

Fructose

Galactose

Glucitol

Glucose

Hexitol

Inversol

Isomalt

Lactose

Malt and maltose

Maltodextrin

Mannitol

Rice syrup solids

Sorbitol

Sucrose

Also, be wary of refined starches, like tapioca starch, potato starch, rice starch, and cornstarch. These ingredients have been stripped of their natural fiber and nutrients so they are almost the same as sugar, as far as your body is concerned.

THE IMPORTANCE OF PURE FOOD

Pure food is vital for a healthy life, for everyone, but especially for a celiac. A strictly 100 percent gluten-free diet, because your life depends on it, can be difficult, now that "gluten-free eating" has become a fad. While gluten can cause inflammation for everyone, and many people without celiac want to eat this way, it can cause confusion. The unfortunate side effect is that many people don't take the necessity for living clean or gluten free seriously. They joke about it, or they just aren't careful, and that can mean you get exposed to gluten. For a serious celiac, that can be especially dangerous—you could be ill for days or even weeks. But even if you don't have celiac disease and you still know you can't or don't want to put gluten or dairy or *anything else* into your body, that's your right too. We know gluten causes inflammation in everyone, not just in those with celiac disease, and we know that many of the people who react to gluten also react to dairy products. We also know that many food additives are harmful, even altering your hormones or brain. So why should you have to be exposed to gluten just because waitstaff, restaurant cooks, food manufacturers, or friends and family don't take your concerns seriously?

It's your health and you get to decide what goes in your body.

The more we talk about this and communicate our concerns and knowledge, the more we hold people accountable and demand clean food that contains what it is supposed to contain and nothing else, the more chance we have of changing attitudes about food purity and improving the health of entire communities.

And if you do get glutened or otherwise "toxified" by some noxious food, I suggest taking some activated charcoal and/or a dairy-free source of acidophilus (a probiotic supplement), drinking tons of water, and sweating it out by taking one of the detox baths on pages 23 and 24 if you are not feeling too weak.

Finding Better Food

Now that you have cleaned up your kitchen, let's replenish it with all the amazing foods that should live there, like fruits, lean meats, and healthy fats. We want to add nutritious foods that support your new healthy life, not detract from it. Getting rid of common inflammatory foods, such as gluten, dairy, soy, refined sugars, and some other items that we will get into later, may feel daunting for some of you. Don't let it. There is a world of food out there that is just waiting for you to discover it, and I am here to help you.

As you venture into this new and exciting way of living, remember that your goal is twofold: (1) You want to eliminate the foods that don't work for you, and (2) you want to add rich, nutrient-dense foods into your diet that give your body more life. Good nutrition is likely what you have been missing. So many people I know don't get enough nutrition from their average diets or don't absorb the nutrients they are taking in.

The best place to start is by first choosing the highest-quality ingredients you can afford (sometimes high-quality whole foods are actually cheaper, like at farmers' markets), then learning to prepare your own healthy and delicious food (with the help of this book). When you can buy organic, buy organic. When you can buy from local farmers, buy from local farmers. When you can grow your own, grow your own. And even if some of these things aren't in your budget, do the best you can. This is a time to choose your foods wisely, not to base your selections on cravings or whims, but on your legitimate and urgent nutritional needs. (I'll talk about those comfort foods and cravings shortly—I'm not asking you to live on vegetables, I promise!)

My best advice for shopping for your particular needs, and the recipes contained in this book, is really universal: When you choose what to eat, don't do it mindlessly. Get the best ingredients you can—fresh, real whole foods that are gorgeous and that excite you—and then always ask yourself before you eat something: Will this nourish me?

When I shop for my own food, I have a few important priorities. I always try to buy 100 percent organic and non-GMO. I understand the cost is more (believe me, I do). My solution is to just buy less of the most expensive products. Think about this: You can buy a ton of junk in bulk at a cheap price

> When you choose what to eat, don't do it mindlessly.

and end up throwing away most of it or making everyone in your household less healthy, or you can buy a precious one-meal's-worth amount of high-quality food that will nourish you and not go to waste. That sounds like a great trade-off to me. I'm serious when I say the chemicals that are put in food these days are a likely contributor to allergies, intolerances, and even autoimmunity. If you don't think about where your food comes from, you are probably inadvertently consuming a lot more of these chemical additives than you realize. We need to get those poisons out of our bodies!

If you don't have a good local source—like Whole Foods, Trader Joe's, local food co-ops, or grocery stores with natural foods sections—to buy your vegetables, fruits, meats, legumes (if you tolerate them), and pantry staples, there are great online sources, like ThriveMarket.com, a new outlet that sells high-quality wholesale items. I buy from FreshDirect.com because of their good selection, but this is only available in the northeast right now. You probably have similar services available to you, so ask around, at your local natural foods store or in groups of like-minded friends. Honestly though, even Walmart has organic food now, and so do most grocery stores. So access to nutrient-dense foods is getting easier, but it can take an extra step or two beyond your regular routine. However, these days, that extra step may be to just head over to the health food aisle or stick to the grocery store periphery where the real food is. Creating new shopping habits will open you up to a whole new world of delicious options that work for your body, not against it.

And while you're in that health food aisle, a warning: Packaged, processed foods labeled "gluten free" and "natural" are not helping you. I understand that sometimes you really need a treat. I get it. This was the hardest part for me after my diagnosis. Until I learned to bake my own treats, my life seemed barren and depressing at times. I feel your pain. But the truth is that those so-called healthy "treats" are usually way overpriced and shockingly nutrient-poor. Instead, make your own treats from whole-food ingredients and keep your refrigerator and freezer stocked with them for those moments when you need a little food love. This book is full of recipes for that exact purpose—so that you could find *both* nutrition and joy, comfort, and solace from your food. I would never tell you that you can't have a cookie or a bagel or a piece of cake, but I will tell you that if you make it yourself with nutrient-dense ingredients and fill it up with love, then it will taste better than anything you could find in the grocery store. It will feed your body and your soul.

YOUR FOOD'S SECRET CODE

Have you ever really looked at the stickers on your produce? Every fruit and vegetable in the grocery store should have a sticker with a PLU code on it, and that code tells you what the food is. The last four numbers are the code for the type of food. If the PLU number has only four digits, it is a conventionally grown product, meaning it is not organic and was likely grown with the use of pesticides. Good to know! When a PLU number has five numbers, you get even more "secret" information. If the first number is an 8, that food is *genetically modified*. If the first number is a 9, that food was *organically grown*. So, look for those 9s! And while GMOs are controversial, my feeling is that until we know more about what they do, it is better to avoid them.

THINK OUTSIDE THE BIG BOX

I love to go to my local farmers' market. Veggies and fruit from nearby are always better than an apple flown in from wherever. Ask the farmers about their process—most really enjoy answering your questions, and I think it's great to support your local farmers. Also, you could see whether your area has a Community Supported Agriculture (CSA) program. This is a great option for eating fresh, local, seasonal food. You pay the farmer at the beginning of the growing season, and every week or so, you get a big box brimming with whatever is currently being harvested. This is a fun way to get creative about what you are going to cook.

Some CSAs also have fresh local meat from small family farms that you can order, sometimes in bulk, to stock your freezer. Some also have fresh eggs (for those of you who can eat them—they are typically not a good idea if you have an autoimmune condition). There are also some suppliers who source quality meat and fish from the region or from small companies with high quality standards, and make deliveries or have monthly pickups. Once you start looking, you might be surprised how much fresh, clean, real food is available to you through alternative channels at a reasonable price.

You could also start your own garden, if you are so inclined. I live in New York City and garden space isn't exactly something everybody has, but even in the city, many people have big pots on their patios with vegetables and fruit growing. Personally, I grow herbs in organic soil on my windowsill to use in cooking—my own miniature herb garden. If you are lucky enough to have an outdoor space, why not give it a try? You could go big if you have the time, or stay small with a tiny plot or containers for vegetables you know you like and eat often. Added benefit: Some people get a lot of stress relief and fresh air from gardening, in addition to the fresh food.

Stocking Your Kitchen with Goodness!

Inspiration is what it's all about! I keep a huge bowl of beautiful in-season fruits and veggies on my counter at all times. The gorgeous colors not only make the room look pretty, but will beg you to eat them. Make your beautiful produce into masterpieces of deliciousness.

For example, an avocado turns into delicious, creamy guacamole. A banana turns into a favorite ingredient in your smoothie, or the batter for my vegan, gluten-free French toast, or a quick snack layered with some nut butter, honey, and cacao nibs! A simple pear can become the main star in a pear crisp or crumble. Keeping these beauties visible makes them super easy to use, and not spoiling in a crisper drawer is only an added bonus.

Take the simple sweet potato, for example. Okay, it may not be the most aesthetically pleasing vegetable in the world, but keeping it on the counter not only makes you use it, but keeps you safe! Did you know that if you store any potato in the refrigerator, once that starch gets chilled, it becomes sugar? This can cause a potentially harmful chemical reaction once you finally get around to cooking them. Chilling also dulls that beautiful potato taste. Sweet potatoes provide a slew of opportunities for deliciousness. Turn them into chips by thinly slicing them, sprinkling with Himalayan salt, and baking at 400°F for 15 minutes or until crispy. Or you can turn them into a savory mash to go with a turkey dinner, or just a simple baked potato that you can enjoy as a snack or part of a meal.

I want you to begin to treat high-quality organic fruits and vegetables as an investment by putting them right in your path. This way, these ingredients won't feel like a burden, something you *have* to eat, but rather what you *get* to eat, as they are displayed for your inspiration and anticipation. I know eating like this can be an investment of your wallet, but I promise the investment into high-quality organic produce is really in the best interest of your well-being and quality of life!

It's all about rethinking your food and recognizing just how important clean eating is.

Now, on to stocking the rest of the kitchen. Our aim is to fill it with foods that are naturally gluten free, dairy free, and anti-inflammatory, and that have great nutritional benefits. If it comes in a box? It's gone. Many of those packaged gluten-free foods are loaded with refined sugar, salt, and ingredients you can't pronounce, which is never a good sign. We are sticking to veggies, fruits, healthy fats, and lean proteins.

I promise—when you have cleaned out the fridge, replenished it with what truly feeds you, and followed my extra tips and items—you will be ready to go. Cooking will become fun again and you will start to realize all the wonderful foods that are just waiting to be rediscovered.

DIY FRUIT AND VEGGIE WASH

If you buy fruits and veggies that aren't organic, always make sure to wash them before putting them in your fruit bowl, so you can grab them and eat them without worrying about washing. You can use simple at-home staples, no chemical cleaners needed. Mix water and baking soda or apple cider vinegar and rinse your produce with it. I even rinse my organic fruits and veggies, just to be sure they don't have anything on the surface.

Sweet potatoes may not be the most aesthetically pleasing vegetable in the world, but maybe keep them in a bowl on your counter anyway to remind you to use them. Great! Now let your creativity flow. Maybe one of those sweet potatoes could take the shape of a chip if sliced thin or maybe another could make a beautiful mash to go with turkey for a holiday dinner, or a baked potato that you can enjoy as a snack or part of a meal.

Or consider bananas, which go brown quickly. Use them up! A simple banana could become a creamy smoothie, a snack when spread with almond butter and sprinkled with cacao nibs, or it could even transform into ice cream by freezing and then puréeing in a high-speed blender with some coconut milk or a little water and ice!

An orange could be segmented and eaten just as is, squeezed into juice, or puréed into a flavorful sauce. The more variety you set out for yourself, the more interesting and nutritious your meals and snacks will become. Don't get boxed in by tradition. Think outside the box and vegetables and fruits will start to seem like the most appealing foods in your kitchen.

My Pantry Staples

One of the best feelings to me is knowing that I have a fully stocked pantry. It makes me confident that I always have something good and safe to eat. A clean, well-stocked pantry is the first step for making the recipes in this book, and it is also the first step into your new, confident life. You won't need everything on this list all at once. You can build up your stock a little at a time, buying a few things whenever you go to the store. These are the pantry, refrigerator, and freezer staples I recommend having around most of the time, that keep me creating every day:

- **APPLE CIDER VINEGAR:** I take this every morning to alkalize the body (see Acid-Balancing Tummy Tonics on page 52).

- **BAKING SODA:** I use baking soda to wash produce, and also mix it into water to drink when I am feeling too acidic.

MY THREE INDISPENSABLE COOKING ESSENTIALS

If you are on a budget or just like to keep things simple, you might be interested in the three things I can't live without when cooking. I use them constantly in almost all the recipes I prepare for myself at home. These are my core staples:

- **OLIVE OIL:** I always have on hand a good-quality organic cold-pressed oil, preferably from a trusted source—since so many big olive oil companies, including some in Europe, have recently been found to be cutting their olive oil with cheaper oils. Whenever I say olive oil in this book, I mean a high-quality extra-virgin olive oil.

- **HIMALAYAN SALT OR OTHER NATURAL SALTS:** There are many kinds of natural salts, but I use Himalayan salt almost exclusively, and it's pretty easy to find now. Pink and rich in minerals, it's a much superior salt to highly processed white table salt. You could also use a good-quality sea salt, if you prefer, or any other of the many kinds of gourmet salts out there. Just read the ingredients and make sure there are no additives.

- **LEMONS:** Preferably organic and unwaxed so you can use the peel for zesting, as appropriate.

You can make pretty much make anything taste good using these three humble ingredients, and you will see them often in this book.

- **BONE BROTH:** I keep individual portions of homemade broth in the freezer; see recipe on page 73.

- **CACAO NIBS, RAW CACAO POWDER, OR ORGANIC COCOA POWDER:** These are all versions of the heart of the cocoa bean. Cacao nibs are broken-up bits of the inner bean, raw cacao powder is this bean ground, and organic cocoa powder is roasted ground beans. They are all nutritious and can be used for various purposes, so I tend to keep them all in my pantry.

- **CINNAMON, GROUND.**

- **COCONUT OIL, PREFERABLY ORGANIC:** Refined is good for cooking and baking when you don't want the coconut flavor. Unrefined or "virgin" coconut oil is less processed and better for when you want that coconut flavor. But you shouldn't heat virgin coconut oil over 350°F, so if you are cooking on higher heat, use refined.

- **GHEE, AKA CLARIFIED BUTTER:** If you are absolutely anti-dairy, you may not want to use ghee, but because the milk solids are taken out and just the clear oil remains, it is much less inflammatory and many people who can't eat any other forms of dairy still eat ghee. It can also be used in cooking at a much higher temperature than regular butter. Even though I am dairy free, I do sometimes make this exception and it doesn't seem to bother me, but I also don't use it very often. Ghee has a delicious buttery taste and it is particularly good on Indian-inspired food. You could make it yourself, but honestly, these days it's available in most grocery stores in the natural foods section, and that makes it a lot easier to have on hand in your refrigerator. Note that ghee is for cooking, not for spreading on food. For spreading, or if you are definitely anti-dairy in every way, see **nondairy butter** later in this list.

- **FISH, FRESH OR FROZEN:** Very nourishing in small amounts.

- **FLOURS FOR BAKING:** I use Jennifer's Way Bakery All-Purpose Flour (I tell you how to make this yourself on page 211, but you can also purchase it on my website), plus specialty flours like almond, coconut, cassava, garbanzo bean, hazelnut, millet, sorghum, and tigernut. You probably won't ever need all of these but, as a baker, the many kinds of specialty flours are interesting to me so I have a lot of them. Just get them as you need them and keep them sealed and refrigerated after opening so they stay fresh. Each one has a different flavor and lends a different character to bakery items. Maybe you will enjoy experimenting.

- **FROZEN FRUIT:** I use fruit for smoothies and always have an assortment in the freezer—get organic if you can.

- **FROZEN VEGETABLES, ORGANIC:** I use these in a pinch when I'm out of every-thing fresh.

- **FRESH GINGER:** This doesn't last forever in the refrigerator so just buy as much as you will use, or do one marathon ginger-grating session and store it in the freezer in small packages of 1 teaspoon or 1 tablespoon, so you have it ready to go when you need it. It's good in both baking and smoothies.

- **GROUND VANILLA BEAN:** I always prefer using fresh ground vanilla, as opposed to vanilla extract. Fresh ground vanilla comes straight from the bean and packs the most vanilla taste, and you can be sure there are no hidden ingredients. You should be able to find it in your local health food market or specialty baking store. You can also purchase it online. Sometimes it is called vanilla powder, but always check the ingredients to be sure there is no added sugar or other additives. It should contain nothing but freshly ground vanilla bean. If you can't find this or don't want to use it, you can always substitute gluten-free vanilla extract, but you will need to double the amount because the taste is less intense and the flavor will never be as good.

- **HEMP MILK (HOMEMADE) OR COCONUT MILK, GUM FREE AND UNSWEETENED:** Occasionally I will use other milks, like unsweetened rice or almond milk, but mostly I default to hemp or coconut. No matter what milk you use, make sure it is free of additives like gums and carrageenan, and unsweetened. When you have the choice, your homemade milks (see page 144) will always be superior to anything processed and in a box or carton.

- **HEMP SEEDS:** If you plan to make your own hemp milk (see page 144), I recommend trying hemp seeds at least once. You can also put a spoonful into a smoothie or sprinkle it over yogurt or add a little to something you are baking, if it agrees with you. I find that when it is ground, it doesn't bother me like some whole seeds sometimes do.

- **HERBS:** I like to have on hand an assortment of organic fresh and dried herbs for seasoning. Again, you won't need everything all at once, so build your herb collection as you need things. When you get any fresh herb, don't use a bit once and then let the rest rot in the crisper. Instead, chop up the entire bunch and freeze it in small labeled packets for future use.

- **HONEY, RAW:** Keep it on the counter but buy it in small batches so it doesn't crystallize. Raw honey retains many more nutrients than more processed types. I particularly like manuka honey.

- **KOSHER SALT:** I usually use kosher salt as a garnish, when I want to see the salt crystals.

- **LIMES:** Buy organic and unwaxed so you can also use the zest for flavoring.

- **MAPLE SUGAR AND COCONUT SUGAR:** I use maple sugar almost exclusively in baking, but it is very expensive and can be hard to find. Coconut sugar also works. If you are okay with it and it doesn't make you feel terrible, you could also use **organic evaporated cane juice** in the recipes in this book, which is a more natural, less processed form of white cane sugar. I do sometimes use evaporated cane juice to make my own powdered sugar (see page 282), but I try not to eat it or bake with it very often. Only you know your own body, though, and how you would react to the occasional use of various types of sweeteners.

- **REAL MAPLE SYRUP:** Organic is best, and grade B is the most flavorful.

- **MEAT, BEEF, CHICKEN, TURKEY, ETC.:** Preferably fresh and organic/free range/grass fed/local, or raised as naturally as possible.

- **NONDAIRY BUTTER:** Earth Balance is a brand of nondairy butter that I trust. It is a lot like margarine but without any milk derivatives or trans fats. You can buy it in sticks for baking or tubs for spreading on toast or muffins. One version has soy, but another version doesn't (in case soy is a problem for you). There are probably other good vegan butter brands, but this one works so well for me that I always use it.

- **NUTS AND SEEDS:** Walnuts, pecans, almonds, pumpkin seeds, sesame seeds, flaxseed, and chia seeds (if you tolerate them) are great for baking but also good in smoothies or to top off recipes.

- **OLIVES:** Look for the jarred kinds from Italy and France, which are much less processed and taste a thousand times better than cheap jarred or canned California olives. Just watch for the pit—you will usually have to spit it out, but it's worth it.

- **PALM SHORTENING:** I often use palm shortening in baking recipes, both for greasing pans and as the fat when it needs to be more solid.

- **PASTA (GLUTEN FREE OF COURSE):** I like Tinkyada and Andean Dream brands, but there are many good choices.

- **PUMPKIN PURÉE:** Because I love to make pumpkin pie (page 65)!

- **RICE:** I use brown short-grain rice for risotto or sushi, basmati rice for coconut rice and Indian-inspired dishes, and jasmine rice for Asian dishes.

- **STARCH (TAPIOCA, ARROWROOT, AND POTATO):** I only use these for baking.

- **TURMERIC:** I get awesome pain relief from this spice—I always add black pepper when using it, to greatly increase the absorption of the helpful compounds.

- **WATER, FRESH AND FILTERED:** If you don't have a water filtration system at home, consider investing in one so your water is as clean as possible. You could also buy spring water or use a filtration pitcher for drinking water.

- **XANTHAN GUM:** This is a powder-like filler that sounds like something chemical or foreign, but it's a simple plant product that stands in very well for eggs in baking, and also gives your baked goods a little more structure that they may be missing without gluten. It works surprisingly well and, while a package seems expensive, it will last a long time because you usually only use a very small amount in any recipe. I use it in any recipe that doesn't use my Jennifer's Way All-Purpose Flour Mix (page 211), because that already contains xanthan gum.

- **YEAST, FOR BAKING:** You could use dry or fresh, but packets of dry are the easiest to use, in my opinion. Just check that they aren't expired, or your bread may not rise.

Kitchen Tools

Cooking is much, much easier if you have a good set of quality tools, appliances, and cooking equipment. Jobs that feel time-consuming and tedious can take just a few minutes and no effort if you have the right equipment. Starting with the right knife, bowls, or saucepan means less mess, time, and frustration. You don't need a lot of things, but if you invest in a few quality tools they can last for years and will come to feel essential in your life.

This is a list of the equipment and tools in my own kitchen that I consider essential, not just for my regular life but for making the recipes in this book. You'll notice it's not long. I don't like to get complicated with a lot of fancy gadgets, and anyway, New York kitchens are tiny so I don't have the space. But these are the things I use nearly every day:

- **CHEF'S KNIFE:** This needs to be good quality and sharp. It should feel comfortable in your hand and make cutting feel easier, not awkward. An awkward-feeling knife is an injury waiting to happen. Some people prefer the feel and balance of a Santoku knife over a chef's knife, so you might want to try them both. Either one will be indispensable for chopping and slicing everything from fruits and vegetables to meat and seafood.

- **HIGH-SPEED BLENDER, SUCH AS A VITAMIX:** This is absolutely essential for making smoothies and puréeing anything liquid. I use mine every day. Cheaper blenders are okay, but more often than not they can't handle the tough jobs and don't truly purée. They also seem to leak. High-speed blenders are more expensive, but they last forever and really do the job right.

- **FOOD PROCESSOR:** A processor is essential for chopping and mixing larger amounts of things like salsa. You can also fly through small jobs like mincing garlic by just popping in the peeled garlic and pulsing a few times—the food processor does all the work. Some also have attachments for grating vegetables (like if you are making coleslaw or zucchini noodles) and juicing citrus fruits. There are some jobs that a food processor really does better than a blender, and it can be easier to get the food out at the end. For small jobs, though, I would usually just use my chef's knife so I don't have a big appliance to clean. You can also get smaller chopper-type versions for doing small jobs like those garlic cloves.

- **STAND MIXER:** I bake a lot, so this is a requirement in my bakery kitchen. I have one with a basic mixing paddle, a wire whip, and a dough hook. KitchenAid is my go-to brand.

- **HAND MIXER:** Sometimes, smaller jobs call for a hand mixer, which is easier to take out and put away than a stand mixer and doesn't require moving everything from a pot or a bowl into the stand mixer bowl. You never technically *have* to have one because you could always use your stand mixer, but you may decide that it is worth the savings in time and effort. I use mine maybe once every week or two.

- **IMMERSION BLENDER:** This wand-like handheld blender will purée soup or sauce right in the pan. This can be easier and safer than using a blender, especially when your soup or sauce is hot.

- **SLOW COOKER:** One of the best inventions ever. Just put your meat and veggies inside, turn it on, and come home at the end of the day to dinner. This is also a super-easy way to make bone broth (page 73) without worrying about watching it constantly.

- **GARLIC PRESS AND POTATO/CARROT PEELER:** Get sturdy ones that won't fall apart in your hands if you use them a lot. Honestly, it's not that much harder to mince garlic with a knife, but a sturdy garlic press can eliminate the peeling step.

- **PASTRY BRUSH:** This is good for brushing melted Earth Balance or ghee on foods, or basting meat. I like a silicone one, which won't leave bristles in your food or melt when exposed to high temps.

- **MEASURING CUPS FOR DRY INGREDIENTS AND WET INGREDIENTS, AND MEASURING SPOONS:** I use dry cups in 1-cup, ½-cup, ⅓-cup, and ¼-cup sizes, as is the standard, as well as the standard measuring spoons. I like steel or wooden ones, personally. For liquid, I have glass measuring cups in 8-cup, 4-cup, 2-cup, and 1-cup sizes. You can eyeball amounts in a lot of recipes, especially things like soup, smoothies, and casseroles, but baking is a science. If you don't measure ingredients for your cakes, cookies, or bread, your recipe might not work.

- **STAINLESS-STEEL COOKWARE:** I thought stainless would be a nightmare to clean, but it's easier than I imagined. Stainless steel heats evenly and is totally inert, so you don't have to worry about weird chemical-based coatings flaking off into your food. Just use lots of delicious ghee, Earth Balance, or coconut oil when you cook and soak the pots and pans immediately after. They come clean easily and you can even put them in the dishwasher. You don't need a huge set. I mostly use a 2-quart saucepan, a large skillet, and a stockpot, all with tight-fitting glass lids so I can see what's going on in the pot.

- **ROASTING PAN:** I mainly use a roasting pan to roast chicken and turkey. I have a heavy-duty cast-iron pan, but you could also use one made of stainless steel. Avoid nonstick pans, which are not only toxic but don't create the juicy bits you can scrape up to make gravy.

- **MIXING BOWLS:** I really only use two, a large bowl and a medium bowl. I think the small ones are too small to be practical for much. I would only use one bowl but often you need to mix dry ingredients in one bowl and wet ingredients in another bowl. An 8-cup glass liquid measuring cup can also double as a mixing bowl.

- **BAKEWARE:** I reach for several key sizes and shapes of baking pans every day. If you like to bake you can't go wrong with a muffin pan for muffins and cupcakes, 8-inch round cake pans (at least 2), loaf pans (regular and mini), a pie dish, an 8-inch-square baking pan, a 9 x 13-inch pan with high sides, a covered baking dish, a sheet cake pan with a rim, and baking sheets. These are the basics, but I do like to collect other things, like larger and smaller cake pans in interesting shapes and sizes, just because I love baking pans. For example, note that a few recipes in this book do require 6-inch cake pans. These are nice to have for small groups because they make a cake that is appropriate for just a few people. Note that some people only like steel bakeware, or stoneware, or glass, or even silicone. I don't use glass as much because it browns too quickly and doesn't come clean very well, but I like both steel and stoneware. Use what you have or find what you prefer. Whatever you get, you will learn with practice whether it works for you.

- **COLANDER AND FINE-MESH STRAINER:** I use these constantly for rinsing vegetables and fruits, draining cans of beans, draining pasta, and straining bone broth. I also sometimes use **cheesecloth** if I need to strain nut milk or anything else where I need an even finer strain than I can get with wire mesh.

- **WOODEN SPOONS, RUBBER SCRAPERS, A WHISK (WIRE OR SILICONE), AND A GOOD STEEL SPATULA:** I keep these in a crock on my counter so they are always handy to grab. I use them all almost every day.

- **MEAT THERMOMETER:** I use my meat thermometer a lot, for both meat and breadmaking.

- **PARCHMENT PAPER:** For lining baking sheets and wrapping up fish for baking.

- **PAPER CUPCAKE/MUFFIN LINERS:** They make it easier to take your cupcakes or muffins with you, and guarantee the bottom half won't get left in the pan. It can be nice to get different colors or designs, especially seasonally.

- **GLASS STORAGE CONTAINERS FOR LEFTOVERS:** These are nice because you can see what's in them, and your food isn't sitting in toxic plastic.

That may seem like a lot, but it's really not if you consider all the gadgets and appliances you *could* buy. Honestly, this is all I ever really use in my very active kitchen, but if there is something else you know you would really use (like a juicer, a tea ball, a spiralizer, a citrus zester, etc.), then definitely add that to your list, and take off anything you know you wouldn't use (like maybe a food processor or an immersion blender). It's your kitchen, your rules, and your tools.

Living Your Life

We are almost ready to dive into the food (it's coming, I promise). I want to talk to you from the deepest part of my heart and tell you that you do not have to live your life not feeling well! I truly believe that, as I live it every day. I have changed my entire world by following my gut, demanding answers for what ailed me, and taking my life and health into my own hands. Doctors are wonderful, but so are our amazing, transformative, self-replenishing bodies. Yours just needs the right fuel to help it heal, grow, and thrive. Whether you deal with celiac disease or another autoimmune disease, or are just so tired of feeling sick and tired, I'm here to tell you that you can change that.

I want to remind you that this is *your* life and *your* health, and you have the right to feel your best. Your body, your health, your journey. You are not alone on this road, either. There are countless people walking around every day existing in pain, frustration, and illness, who have just accepted this as their reality. It *doesn't have to be*. Seek out supportive people who also demand change in their lives and start this journey with them. Having a friend to share the experience with is always a plus. Come join my Facebook community, Jennifer's Way Bakery, or come visit me on my website, LivingFreeJennifer.com, and find a wonderful community waiting for you to share stories, ideas, issues, and recipes with. You are not alone in your search for better! I'm here, as are many others. I hope this book excites you about the possibilities of food that can directly affect your well-being. You have endless possibilities to make your life delicious again.

Okay, now let's get in the kitchen and let's eat!

Pure

RECIPES FOR HEALING

*W*elcome to a whole new world of food. If you have been having health issues, or just generally feeling inflamed or off, you may be wondering what the heck you could eat that might actually make you feel better. Feeling better and still eating well are the goals of this section of the book. Whether you have celiac disease or another autoimmune disorder, or you just want to feel great, this is your chance to start healing. Everyone can benefit from the eating style of this chapter, which is all about an anti-inflammatory approach to living. Pure is the place to start on the path to resetting your health.

I learned to eat this way not, as you might expect, after my diagnosis with celiac disease, but after years of already living gluten free and dairy free. Three years after my diagnosis, I hit a wall. My autoimmune disease was getting out of control again and my inflammation was at an all-time high. I had dark circles under my swollen eyes. I was exhausted and moody, had severe headaches and body aches, my hair was falling out, and I was gaining weight for no apparent reason. That's when I came across the Autoimmune Protocol (AIP) diet, which eliminates all grains, and much much more. It is very strict but it allows the body to heal while slowly incorporating other foods back in. It's a process, but it worked for me. I use some of those principles in this section of the book. If you have severe celiac disease or another autoimmune disease and you are already eating gluten and dairy free but still having problems, I would definitely focus on eating from the Pure recipes (you might also check out the AIP—start here: www.saragottfriedmd.com/is-the-autoimmune-protocol-necessary). If this level of strictness appeals to you (and it certainly helps me when I need to get my health back on track), these recipes will help you do that.

There have been many other times that I've needed to return to Pure eating, including a period where my inflammation became extreme and I couldn't seem to get past it for many weeks. At last I found out that I had some cancerous changes in some breast cells. My body had been telling me something was wrong, but it took a long time for the doctors to figure out what it was. Fortunately it all turned out okay, but it was a long and painful time, and eating Pure really helped get me through it.

As you know, every recipe in this book is already free of gluten, dairy, eggs, refined sugar, alcohol, and food additives, but the recipes in this section are *also* free of:

- **ALL GRAINS** (not just the ones with gluten)

- **LEGUMES**

- **NUTS AND SEEDS**

- **NIGHTSHADE VEGETABLES:** tomatoes, white and yellow potatoes, all types of peppers, eggplant, goji berries

- **RAW VEGETABLES,** which I find very hard to digest when I'm inflamed

In my experience, this is the absolute best way to nurture yourself. It may sound strict at first, but when you get to the actual recipes, you will see how much you can eat, and how enjoyable eating can be, even without those foods you might be eating daily. Especially if you are newly diagnosed or simply giving your system a little extra TLC so your gut can heal and you can regain your strength and energy, cutting back strictly on things that tend to be inflammatory can make a big difference, and is totally worthwhile. When you are feeling stronger, you can move on to the Clean section and introduce some foods back into your diet. For me, sometimes I can handle non-gluten grains in small amounts, or some tomatoes, or almonds. But I don't go overboard, and if I start feeling inflamed again, I rush right back here to Pure.

You will find many ways to make filling and delicious meals and snacks in the Pure recipes. You'll even find dessert (you'll love the one made out of avocado) and bread! (It's true—you don't need grain to make bread. I never would have believed it if I hadn't made it myself.) Every recipe in Pure is particularly gentle, digestible, soothing, and nutrient-rich without containing anything inflammatory. Stay with these recipes until your digestion begins to heal and you feel stronger and less inflamed. At that point, you can try some of the recipes in the Clean and Indulgent sections, where we work some of those safer ingredients back in.

I also recommend keeping a food journal during the time you are eating Pure. Track how you feel at the end of each day, or even at the end of each meal. Then look back after a week and see if it has made a difference for you. I'll tell you this: Two friends recently visited for a long weekend. One is a celiac, and the other is not. They both loved the food I was making for them all weekend, and both commented on how great they felt. They didn't even know they were eating Pure. They just knew they liked the feeling so much that they both wanted to keep eating that way at home. I gave them the guidelines and within ten days, both said they noticed decreased swollen eyes and decreased inflammation overall; and they both lost about six pounds. Three months later, they are still eating this way, dipping into Clean at times, and also Indulgent at times, but mostly staying with Pure...and enjoying every moment of it.

Note that, for me, eating Pure is never about weight loss, but a lot of other people tell me they lose weight. So if that is something you are trying to do, it may help. Also, and this is very important (don't hate me): No alcohol, no soda *ever*, and no drinks with added sugar or caffeine, except green tea, which is quite anti-inflammatory. You may not like it for a day or two, but then you will be so glad you put those inflammatory substances behind you.

As you will soon discover, eating is a balancing act of self-care and pleasure, as well as self-awareness, because if you don't pay attention to how you feel on any given day, you will be less able to make the right choices for you and your health. Sometimes, your symptoms will flare, and you may or may not know why. Sometimes you will wake up feeling like a superhero. Eat to honor yourself, rather than ignoring your body's daily status, and you will be eating to heal and thrive.

Pure Tonics and Smoothies

Start your day gently with soothing tonics to ease your digestion into action. The healing liquids won't irritate your gut, and the whole day will go more smoothly. Whenever I'm feeling in need of healing, I wake up with a tonic.

And smoothies are a great morning option when you're in healing mode, or in any mode really. Loaded with vitamins and nutrients, smoothies are easy to absorb because they are liquefied. Easy absorption is essential for anyone dealing with a gut that doesn't absorb nutrients very well, as is the case with those who have celiac disease, especially in the early stages. I always recommend making smoothies yourself because most of the ones you buy or order from restaurants are full of sugar. With homemade smoothies, you know exactly what is in them and exactly how much of the ingredients. The smoothies in this section are particularly soothing and anti-inflammatory.

THIS DRINK SAVED MY LIFE! Okay, I may be exaggerating slightly, but it sure felt like it at the time. I was having extreme inflammation in my gut that caused painful pressure all the way up through my chest. When I went to see a wonderful acupuncturist, he introduced me to a tea, which I then tweaked and came up with this soothing, warm drink. I drank it every single day for a month. The pressure in my chest subsided almost immediately. What caused it? Who knows: When you have an autoimmune disease, you don't always know *why* your body reacts the way it does. All I know is that my morning tonic was like turning a fire extinguisher on a kitchen fire. Sometimes I also have it after a big meal, to improve digestion, but I especially recommend it as the first thing you put into your body in the morning.

The tea can be made and then put in the refrigerator if you like it cold, or enjoyed warm or at room temperature.

Serves 1 or 2

1 teaspoon fennel seeds

1 teaspoon ground ginger

1 teaspoon ground turmeric

2 cups filtered water

Fresh lemon juice and raw honey, to taste (optional)

Morning Tonic

Combine all the ingredients in a small saucepan and bring just to a boil. Strain into a mug and drink as is, or add some fresh-squeezed lemon and raw honey. (I like Manuka honey.)

Note that the tonic includes fennel seeds, but because they are strained and you aren't eating the actual seed, they will not be irritating.

ACID-BALANCING TUMMY TONICS

Alkalize your body and give your liver and kidneys a good flush with two simple, quick, practically effortless acid-balancing tonics, outlined here. I recommend starting your day with one before putting anything else in your body. Both are hydrating, nourishing, and incredibly effective at reducing acid in the body. An alkalized body can better absorb vital nutrients so you can stay stronger, physically and mentally, and is also crucial for gut health. And both remedies are particularly effective if you have an acid stomach, such as from heartburn or reflux. They also seem to boost immunity—I believe they are what keep me healthy when everyone around me is catching cold viruses. Okay, they aren't the best-tasting remedies in the world, but when you will do anything to combat stomach acid, they are worth it. I suggest trying them both (not at the same time, but on different days), and seeing which taste you prefer and which works best for you. They are both simple to prepare, and I highly recommend them:

- Mix 1 teaspoon baking soda into 1 cup filtered water until dissolved, then drink.

- Mix 1 teaspoon raw apple cider vinegar into 1 cup warm filtered water, then drink. (It may sound counterintuitive to say that vinegar reduces acid since it is an acid, but in the body it seems to have an acid-lowering effect. It certainly works well for me.)

WHAT BETTER WAY to brighten your day and your mood than with some vitamin C? It helps tissues heal faster, so it's perfect for anyone focusing on gut healing. Drink this fruity C-rich drink fresh, or pour into an ice cube tray and freeze for a snack (like little potent healing ice pops). Vitamin C + happiness = Sunshine in a Glass!

Note that while the recipe calls for fresh juice from an orange and a lemon, and you may be able to get this easily at a juice bar, you could also use the whole fruits, if you want to get more of the nutritious pulp. Just peel off the skins, pick out the seeds, and drop the rest into the blender—but peel over the blender or over a bowl to catch any stray juice, so you don't waste a precious drop.

Serves 1

1 apple, peeled, cored, and coarsely chopped

Juice of 1 large orange, or ½ cup fresh orange juice

Juice of 1 lemon

½-inch piece fresh ginger, peeled and cut into slices

¼ teaspoon ground turmeric

Sunshine in a Glass

Combine all the ingredients in a high-speed blender and blend until fully combined. Drink up and feel happy!

VARIATION You can use any sunshine-y fresh fruit in this recipe. Try replacing the apple with 1 cup of papaya, mango, peach, or nectarine cubes.

TURMERIC is of huge benefit when you are attempting to reduce inflammation. It's an intense antioxidant, offering many beneficial compounds for gut healing, and has also been found to help level out thyroid function, which can't hurt, even if you think your thyroid is fine. Black pepper may seem out of place in a breakfast tonic, but it actually helps the body absorb much more of the healing properties of the turmeric. The creamy coconut milk is also great for your brain (you could also use any other plant milk that you tolerate). Served warm in a big mug, this creamy and savory-sweet turmeric milk, sometimes called "golden milk," also works great any time of day. So give it a try for breakfast, or as a soothing before-bed drink.

Serves 2

1 (15-ounce) can full-fat organic coconut milk with no additives or fillers

1¼ cups filtered water

1 teaspoon coconut oil

1 tablespoon ground turmeric, or 1-inch piece fresh turmeric, grated (fresh turmeric is easy to find in health food stores now, and I much prefer fresh to ground in this recipe)

1 teaspoon ground cinnamon

Pinch of freshly ground black pepper

About 1 tablespoon raw honey, or to taste

Warming Turmeric Milk

Combine the coconut milk, water, coconut oil, turmeric, cinnamon, and pepper in a small saucepan and whisk together until combined (you could also use an immersion blender). Heat over medium heat until simmering, about 5 minutes. Pour into two mugs, sweeten with honey, and enjoy. You can also drink one mug and reserve the other half for the evening or the next morning. It will keep fine in the refrigerator.

I REMEMBER during the first couple of months after diagnosis, I literally drank all of my meals because my gut didn't want to digest anything. For me, smoothies were perfect for supplying nutrients while letting my gut rest, and this one in particular felt extremely nourishing and anti-inflammatory on my worst days.

The smoothie is boosted with bovine gelatin, which you could add to any smoothie you invent. Bovine gelatin is full of collagen, which is great for gut healing. Just make sure your gelatin comes from a good organic source, preferably grass-fed cows, and doesn't contain any added sweeteners. You can find bovine gelatin in health food stores or online. There are several good brands, even vegan brands that use plant ingredients similar to gelatin; I use the organic Great Lakes brand.

If you want to make this smoothie more like a milk shake, use a frozen banana and/or 1 cup frozen peaches. You could also add a few ice cubes in with the water.

Gut-Healing Smoothie

Serves 1 or 2

1 ripe banana, peeled

1 peach, pitted and cut into chunks

1 orange, peeled, segmented, and pitted

Juice of 1 lemon

1 tablespoon bovine gelatin

½ to 1 cup water or plain unsweetened coconut water (enough for it to mix together smoothly)

Put everything into a high-speed blender, blend until smooth, and enjoy.

BOVINE GELATIN AND BOVINE COLLAGEN

Bovine gelatin and bovine collagen are both made from the bones and skin of cows, and they are both health-boosting products that you can add to smoothies and fruit bowls to help with bone and joint pain, gut healing, and even younger-looking skin. As they are used in this book, they can be used interchangeably. The only difference is that in bovine collagen powder, the proteins are broken down into smaller pieces, so it is even easier to digest. Also, bovine collagen powder dissolves more easily in cold liquid and does not have a gelling effect. Otherwise, they are pretty much interchangeable unless you actually want the gelling effect. I use both of them, but if you only want to spring for one of them, I would pick the bovine collagen powder, which you should be able to find in health food stores or online.

Pure Breakfasts or Anytime Snacks

When I'm eating pure, I focus on the most gentle, anti-inflammatory foods I can have, that will still make me feel content and happy. Remember, this is not about depriving yourself. It's all about rethinking your food. For example, you may think raw vegetables are healthy—well, yes, but they are also really hard on the digestive system. On the other hand, fruit is highly anti-inflammatory and soothing. It's a perfect remedy for those high-inflammation days (or weeks). It's about keeping your system calm and keeping inflammation at bay. Pure meals, like muffins, cacao pudding, grain-free biscuits, even my pumpkin pie and homemade Turkey-Apple Breakfast Sausage are all items you would never think would be okay to keep inflammation down and your gut happy, but they are. I often enjoy all of these favorite foods for breakfast, but I also enjoy them for snacks, lunch, or any other time I need Pure nourishment. Meals shouldn't be about labels. They should be about what you want and need when you are hungry.

HERE IS ANOTHER LOVE OF MINE! Acai is a berry with powerful antioxidants that also happens to be delicious, especially in this pudding-like breakfast (or anytime) snack. When purchasing acai berry purée, make sure it is unsweetened, as many brands add a ton of sugar. I like to mix my daily powdered vitamins and extra vitamin C powder into the blend and, sometimes, some bovine collagen powder, just to really make this into an anti-inflammatory power meal.

For toppings, I like blueberries, blackberries, raspberries, coconut flakes, cacao nibs, and some coconut nondairy yogurt. Although they are nightshades, I sometimes add a few dried goji berries, which don't seem to bother me. For you, get creative and go for whatever toppings and fruits make you smile and feel well. This is your bowl!

Serves 1 or 2

Acai Bowl

1 cup organic frozen fruit of any kind—especially berries

1½ frozen bananas, peeled

1 (3- to 5-ounce) package unsweetened acai purée (if frozen, hold under warm water for 3 minutes and break up by hand before opening)

¼ cup frozen organic blueberries

1 tablespoon fresh lemon juice

1 date, pitted

¼ cup liquid (your choice of water, juice, Homemade Hemp Milk (page 144), or other unsweetened nondairy milk of choice) or nondairy yogurt

Suggested toppings: unsweetened shredded coconut, goji berries (if you tolerate them), fresh blueberries, sliced banana, strawberries, and/or peaches, blackberries, cacao nibs, raisins or nuts (if you're not eating Pure), or whatever else you can imagine

Put all the fruit (except toppings) in a high-speed blender. Add the liquid or yogurt and blend until the mixture is a creamy, thick consistency. Pour into a large bowl and top with your choice of goodies.

I THOUGHT YOU SAID "NO NUTS AND SEEDS"

If you are eagle-eyed, you may have noticed that I said this chapter contains no nuts or seeds, but sometimes you will see things like hemp milk or other nondairy milks, which might include almond milk, hazelnut milk, flax milk, or something similar. The reason I don't include nuts and seeds in this chapter is because they are very difficult to digest. When puréed and made into milk, however, the indigestible parts are filtered out, so these nut and seed milks are just fine when you are eating Pure.

I CREATED THIS one morning when the only food I had in the house was some bananas. The fruit bowl has now become one of my all-time favorite breakfasts or snacks. The flavor of banana mixed with cinnamon and the sweetness of honey, all countered by the salt, makes me happy. I love cinnamon and use it every chance I get. Not only is it delicious, but it's one of the healthiest spices you can put on your food: It's loaded with antioxidants and has anti-inflammatory properties, which is why you will see it in many of the recipes in this book. I also love honey, which also has great antioxidant properties as well as antifungal properties, so it's great for the digestive tract. I thought, what the heck, let me combine them. When in season, you could also add other fruits to make a fancier, if a little more time-consuming, fruit bowl. Try strawberries, blackberries, raspberries, peach slices, or even my very favorite fruit—fresh figs!

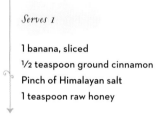

Serves 1

1 banana, sliced
½ teaspoon ground cinnamon
Pinch of Himalayan salt
1 teaspoon raw honey

Quick Banana Pick-Me-Up

Arrange the banana slices (and other fruit, if you like) on a plate and sprinkle with the cinnamon and salt. Drizzle with the raw honey. *Yum!*

I USED TO GO grain free only when I was feeling my worst, but these days I pretty much go with it all the time, just because I feel so much better—never bloated or overly full or any of those other things that happen when your body sets off alarms to let you know it doesn't like what you just ate. I think that I would have a much harder time doing this, however, if it weren't for baked treats like these muffins. Kids in particular love them. They taste like "real" muffins (and of course they *are* real muffins). I swear that once you make them you will be baking and eating muffins weekly.

If you'd like to add some variety to your muffin game, change up the flavor by substituting ½ cup pumpkin or sweet potato purée for the banana. And don't hesitate to double the recipe if you want to make a dozen muffins. What I love most about the muffins is their portability: Put them in a zippered plastic bag, throw in your bag or your child's lunch box, and enjoy them on the go.

Grain-Free Vanilla Banana Muffins

Makes 6 muffins

¾ cup coconut flour

½ cup cassava flour

¼ cup tigernut flour

½ cup arrowroot starch

½ cup maple sugar, date sugar, or coconut sugar

1 teaspoon aluminum-free baking powder

1 teaspoon baking soda

½ teaspoon xanthan gum

½ teaspoon ground cinnamon

½ teaspoon Himalayan salt

1 very ripe banana

¼ cup unsweetened applesauce

1 teaspoon ground vanilla bean (or 2 teaspoons gluten-free vanilla extract)

⅓ cup coconut oil

¾ cup coconut milk

TIGERNUT FLOUR

Tigernut flour is a gluten-free flour made from a root. It has fiber, protein, and a lot of vitamins and minerals, including iron and magnesium.

Preheat the oven to 350°F. Line a standard 6-cup muffin pan with baking liners.

Whisk together all the dry ingredients (through salt) in a large mixing bowl. In a separate bowl with a stand mixer or a hand mixer, combine the banana, applesauce, vanilla, and oil until smooth. A little at a time, add the flour mixture, alternating with the coconut milk and mixing slowly as you go. Mix until smooth and fully blended.

Divide the batter evenly among the baking liners. Bake for 20 to 30 minutes, until a toothpick inserted into the center of a muffin comes out clean. Let sit for at least 20 minutes before eating. Garnish with a slice of banana and a sprinkle of cinnamon. Store in an airtight container on the counter for up to 2 days.

SERIOUSLY, I eat this pie for breakfast, lunch, dinner, and dessert. And why not? There is no refined sugar, and it's pumpkin, which is loaded with fiber, vitamin A, amino acids, and zinc. It's a simple treat that shouldn't be just for dessert. It has saved me on more than one occasion when I was in serious need of something carb-y and sweet. It's simply the best. Serve at a holiday dinner, bring it to a potluck, or just eat it because you want it. There's simply no reason not to enjoy this pie frequently.

Serves 4

The Breakfast, Lunch, Dinner, or Dessert Pumpkin Pie

Grain-Free Piecrust (page 102)

1 (15-ounce) can organic pumpkin purée

¼ cup full-fat canned coconut milk

¼ cup real maple syrup

Splash of fresh orange juice

1 tablespoon plus 1 teaspoon arrowroot starch

1 teaspoon xanthan gum

2 teaspoons ground vanilla bean (or 4 teaspoons gluten-free vanilla extract)

¾ teaspoon ground cinnamon

½ teaspoon ground or freshly grated nutmeg

½ teaspoon ground ginger

¼ teaspoon ground cloves

1 teaspoon Himalayan salt

Preheat the oven to 350°F. Prebake the crust for about 10 minutes, until warm and firm. Let sit for a few minutes to cool. Keep the oven on.

Combine all the remaining ingredients in a large bowl and mix with a spoon or hand mixer.

Spoon the pumpkin mixture into the pie shell. Bake for about 30 minutes, until the pie is somewhat firm to the touch (it will get firmer as it cools). This is a grain-free crust so it won't brown. (But if you'd like to brown it slightly, rub some coconut oil or nondairy butter around the edges of the crust when there's 10 minutes to go, but watch carefully because you don't want it to burn.) Let the pie sit for 25 minutes. I like to place it in the refrigerator to really firm up and cool—for that familiar pumpkin pie texture. Store leftovers covered in the refrigerator for up to 2 days.

WHILE BRIEFLY STAYING in L.A. with a friend, another dear old friend of mine invited me over to catch up. I have never seen this friend without also bringing something I made to eat. She has children who had been to the bakery, and they love what I bake, so the thought of walking in empty-handed just didn't sit well with me. I only had an hour before I had to leave, so I didn't have time to bake anything. What to do? Pudding! What kid doesn't like pudding? I spotted some very ripe avocados on the counter and got to work.

As I walked in that day to greet my friend, her kids spotted the Mason jars. They whisked them away from me and started devouring them. My friend looked at me like, "Really? You brought them sugar?" I whispered in her ear that her children were currently stuffing themselves with avocado. She couldn't believe it.

I think you will love this dessert as much as my friend's kids, and if you serve it to family or guests I can almost guarantee that they will have no idea what the secret ingredient is. As for the add-ins? Simply layer the pudding with fruit of your choice, cacao nibs, or coconut. If you are eating Clean, you could add dairy-free chocolate chips, nut butter, granola, or gluten-free marshmallows.

Makes 3 medium-size Mason jars, depending on how much you add in additional toppings

Raw Cacao Pudding in Mason Jars

4 very ripe avocados, pitted and peeled

3 dates, pitted

1 ripe banana

3/4 to 1 1/2 cups raw cacao powder (more or less to taste, depending on how chocolaty you like it)

1/4 to 1/2 cup real maple syrup, more or less to taste

1/4 cup full-fat canned coconut milk or other nondairy milk of choice (may need more liquid if it's too thick for the blender, but be careful not to add too much liquid; you want to make sure it stays nice and thick, like pudding)

1/2 to 1 teaspoon ground coffee

1/2 teaspoon Himalayan salt

1/2 teaspoon ground cinnamon

1/2 teaspoon ground vanilla bean (or 1 teaspoon gluten-free vanilla extract)

Blend all the ingredients in a high-speed blender, starting slow and then going faster. Taste as you go to check for sweetness and consistency, and adjust seasonings as needed.

Spoon the pudding into Mason jars, layering with add-ins if you like, and serve. The pudding will keep, sealed in the jars, for up to 3 days in the refrigerator.

COCOA OR CACAO?

I always prefer to use raw cacao powder rather than cocoa powder because it is a less processed, more natural product. Raw cacao powder is made from unroasted, cold-pressed cocoa beans, so the fat is removed but all the other enzymes and phytochemicals remain, and it is a great source of antioxidants and magnesium. Raw cacao nibs are little pieces of this inner bean and are a serious upgrade from processed chocolate chips. Cocoa powder is like the cooked version—it is roasted at high temperatures so it's got an extra processing step. It's still a potent source of some good nutrients, and it costs a lot less, so if that's all you have, don't feel bad about using it—although I definitely recommend using an organic version.

THESE BISCUITS have become my savior. It took a very, *very* long time to get them right and, to this day, I continue to tweak the recipe to make them even better. I came up with the biscuits when I was in bad shape from some extreme inflammation. The only way I felt any relief was by eating a completely grain-free diet with no sugar, and very small meals.

Now, this was seriously, truly difficult for me because one of my favorite foods in the world is the starchy gluten-free bread that took me years to perfect. I was very attached to it, but at that difficult time, I knew I had to go grain free for a while. Then again, this was just another challenge for me; I had my mission. I went into the kitchen and tried and tried, and tried again to make a substitute that would satiate my desire for a soft, warm piece of bread. The many inedible creations I came up with at first led me to believe it just wasn't going to be possible to have bread in my mouth. But then, a biscuit miracle. One day I somehow stumbled upon the exact right amount of each ingredient and out of nowhere, it just worked. The biscuit gods smiled upon me.

I have made these for everyone: children and adults, celiacs and non-celiacs; *everyone* loves them. Serve them warm with coconut butter and honey—you can thank me later.

Makes 8 biscuits

½ cup cassava flour
⅓ cup coconut flour
½ cup arrowroot starch
1 teaspoon aluminum-free baking powder
¼ teaspoon xanthan gum
¼ teaspoon Himalayan salt
¾ cup filtered water
¼ cup coconut oil or olive oil
1 teaspoon raw honey (optional)
1 teaspoon baking soda
1 tablespoon apple cider vinegar or fresh lemon juice
¼ cup unsweetened applesauce (or 2 tablespoon chia seeds mixed with ¼ cup warm water, if you are eating from the Clean section of this book)

Grain-Free Biscuits

Preheat the oven to 350°F. Line a baking sheet with parchment paper.

In a large mixing bowl, combine the cassava flour, coconut flour, starch, baking powder, xanthan gum, and salt. In a separate bowl, combine the water, coconut oil, and honey. Add the wet ingredients to the dry, mixing as you go.

In another small bowl, combine the baking soda and vinegar, then mix into the dough. Finally, add the applesauce or chia seed mixture and mix until everything is combined.

Drop 8 large spoonfuls of the dough onto the lined baking sheet. Bake until golden-brown, 15 to 20 minutes. Serve warm.

The biscuits will keep in an airtight container for about 1 day, or for a couple of weeks in the freezer.

WHEN I WAS A KID, sausage dipped in maple syrup was always such a treat at breakfast. When my celiac disease was first diagnosed, I was told that eating sausage was a no-no because purchased sausage usually has fillers and sausage casings are often a prime place for hidden gluten. Bummer...until I decided to make dreams happen and make my own. These sausages are delicious on their own for a hearty breakfast or as a midday snack, and they are gentle enough on your gut so that digestion isn't an issue.

Serves 4

1 teaspoon olive oil

1 small shallot, minced

1 apple, peeled, cored, and chopped

¼ cup unsweetened applesauce

1 teaspoon real maple syrup (plus more for dipping, optional)

1 pound ground turkey

1 tablespoon chopped fresh Italian parsley

1 teaspoon Himalayan salt

1 teaspoon freshly ground black pepper

Turkey–Apple Breakfast Sausage

Preheat the oven to 400°F. Line a baking sheet with parchment paper.

Coat a skillet with the olive oil and warm over medium-high heat until you can smell the aroma. Add the shallot and cook until translucent, about 5 minutes. Add the apple and stir to mix with the shallot. Add the applesauce and maple syrup and cook until the apple is tender, about 5 minutes. Transfer to a bowl and set aside to cool.

In a separate bowl, combine the turkey, parsley, salt, and pepper. Add the cooled apple mixture, mixing everything together with your hands. Form into 8 patties and place on the lined baking sheet. Bake until cooked through and sizzling, 20 to 25 minutes. Serve hot, with maple syrup for dipping if you like.

Pure Soups and Broth

Just as with smoothies, broths and soups (especially puréed soups) do some of the digesting work for you, so you can take in the nutrients without overtaxing your gut. I drink a lot of bone broth and have soup often when I'm eating Pure, and I can practically feel the nutrients I'm absorbing. I'm also a huge puréed soup fan, especially in cold months. What's better than a thick, warm soup on a bitter-cold day, especially when you don't even have to chew it? For me, a rich, nutrient-dense soup that eats like a meal and has just a handful of ingredients is a win-win. Plus, most take only 15 to 20 minutes to make—a plus for anyone who needs to let their bellies rest for a moment but is in no mood for complicated cooking.

IT'S NOT AS STRANGE as it used to be. Now that bone broth is getting a lot more coverage in health news, people don't think it's so weird, but I remember the days when the name alone made people say "no thanks." In fact, that was me for years, until I read an article about how healing it is for the gut lining and how it is a potent source of minerals, which can be difficult to get from many foods and are often deficient in people with digestive issues. I decided to bite the bullet and give it a try, and now it's a regular part of my routine.

Basically, making bone broth is a slow-cooking process that pulls minerals out of the bones and collagen out of the connective tissue of a chicken carcass or other animal bones. The resulting broth helps repair your gut lining, improves your skin with a collagen infusion, and delivers minerals that help your body work better and heal. Bone broth is also immune boosting and anti-inflammatory.

Because so much of the bone and tissue dissolves into this broth, it is absolutely essential that you use the best possible bones you can find—they should be from organically raised, grass-fed or free-range, GMO-free, clean animals. Any pesticides, chemicals, or drugs used on or fed to the animal could concentrate in your bone broth, making it toxic instead of healing. In the end, whatever the animal has ingested is in its bones—so make sure you'd want that in your body too.

The broth takes a good 24 hours to make, but you don't have to watch it if you use a slow cooker. When my gut needs extra support, I leave bone broth cooking in the slow cooker and ladle some out to drink several times each day, until it is gone.

If you don't have a slow cooker, you can simmer the broth in a stockpot over low heat on the stovetop, or bring it to a simmer on the stove and then let it cook in a 200°F oven partially covered for up to 24 hours (if you have an oven-safe pot), but both methods require more vigilance than a slow cooker. Are you comfortable falling asleep with the stove or the oven on? I wouldn't be, so the slow cooker is my standby.

The recipe calls for a chicken carcass. I typically use the carcass left over from a small roasted chicken. After removing the meat for another meal, I just put the bones and veggies in the slow cooker, cover with water, and let it go. You could use a turkey carcass, but if it is too big to fit in the cooker you'll need to break it in half and freeze half for a future batch. You can also substitute other animal bones like beef knuckle bones and marrow bones (particularly rich in collagen), or lamb bones. Don't worry if the bones break and

Bone Broth

⟶ recipe continues

marrow gets into the broth—this will just make it more nutritious. You can also make seafood bone broth with fish bones and shrimp shells. Basically, if you have bones or shells lying around, don't waste them. Get the minerals out by making bone broth.

If you've never had bone broth, you may be surprised that when chilled, a good long-simmered bone broth will sometimes firm up into a jelly-like substance, rather than staying liquid. This is a good sign that your broth is rich with collagen. It will melt back into a liquid when you reheat it. If it doesn't turn jelly-like, that's okay too. It will still be rich with minerals.

Makes about 8 cups

1 organic chicken carcass, or 2 to 3 pounds of other bones from organically raised, grass-fed/pastured animals (or fish bones, shellfish shells, and/or shrimp shells)

1 large onion, quartered (no need to peel it)

3 small carrots, cut into large chunks

3 stalks celery, cut into large chunks

A few sprigs of parsley

4 cloves garlic, peeled and cut in half or crushed

1 bay leaf (dried or fresh)

2 tablespoons apple cider vinegar (this helps pull the nutrients out of the bones)

Filtered water (enough to cover the carcass)

CHICKEN FOOT SOUP?

Some people add chicken feet to their bone broth because chicken feet have a high concentration of collagen, which is great for your joints and skin. You can probably get a bundle from your butcher. Some stores even carry them next to the organ meats. If you can find good clean organic chicken feet and can get past the "I'm putting feet in my soup" factor, I recommend using them. If you do, your bone broth will almost certainly turn jelly-like when chilled. Believe it or not, people used to eat it that way, slurping it up with a spoon like meat gelatin (they called it aspic).

In a slow cooker (or large pot on the stove if you are going to watch it), combine the chicken carcass or other bones and all the other ingredients and cover with filtered water. Turn the slow cooker on low (if using the stove, bring to a boil, then lower the heat all the way down to low and leave partially covered). Let the bone broth cook for 24 hours. Check and stir every so often, skimming any foam off the top.

After the 24 hours are up, pour the contents of the slow cooker (or pot) through a fine-mesh strainer into a large bowl. Return just the broth to the slow cooker or pot. Ladle broth into a cup or bowl and enjoy the heavy-duty healing! You can also use bone broth to enrich any soup recipe—just add it in place of water. You can also use it in place of water to make risotto.

I store my bone broth in Mason jars in the refrigerator, where it will keep for about a week. You could also freeze it (in 1- or 2-cup servings, or in ice cube trays), where it will keep for about a month.

THERE ARE FEW THINGS more healing than a good chicken soup, and this one is perfect for when you have a cold or the flu and need nourishment but you can hardly breathe or taste anything. It will soothe your throat, calm your stomach, and help kick your immune system into high gear. Just be sure you have homemade bone broth at the ready. That's why I like to have some on deck all winter long.

I often make the soup the day after having roast chicken and making bone broth. It's a great way to use up the leftovers and take advantage of the bone broth when it's just ready. If you don't have leftover chicken, you can just chop up a chicken breast and sauté it with the onions. If you are congested, don't leave out the cayenne pepper. Technically, it is a nightshade, but the amount here is so small and it is so good at clearing your sinuses that I think it's worthwhile, unless you know it definitely aggravates you.

Jennifer's Way Cold-and-Flu-Fighting, Winter-Ready Chicken Soup

Serves 4

1 tablespoon olive oil

1 medium onion, chopped

2 cloves garlic, minced

2 stalks of celery, sliced

1 carrot, chopped

1 cup shredded cooked chicken (or 1 raw chicken breast, cut into cubes)

4 cups Bone Broth (page 73)

1 tablespoon chopped fresh Italian parsley

2 teaspoons Himalayan salt

1 teaspoon dried oregano

1/2 teaspoon dried thyme

1/2 teaspoon freshly ground black pepper

1/4 teaspoon cayenne pepper

Heat the olive oil in a large saucepan over medium-high heat and sauté the onion until soft, about 8 minutes. Add the garlic, stir, and cook for an additional 2 minutes. Add the celery and carrot and cook for an additional 3 minutes. Add the chicken and toss to coat with the onions and garlic. Add the bone broth, parsley, salt, oregano, thyme, black pepper, and cayenne. Bring to a boil, reduce the heat to medium-low, and simmer, covered, for at least 30 minutes or up to 1 hour. Serve warm.

You could also put everything into the slow cooker and cook for up to 8 hours on low, which is nice if you have to work all day. Coming home to warm chicken soup is a lovely feeling, especially if winter is getting the best of you.

I HAVE A DEEP LOVE for olive oil. For Christmas, a dear friend of mine gave me the perfect gift—a monthly delivery of different flavors of oil. *Wonderful!* One month I received a perplexing bottle of mint oil and couldn't figure out how to use its unique flavor. It didn't quite work with any of my standby meals.

Then one afternoon, I was making my favorite creamy broccoli soup. (When you try it, you will love how creamy it is without any dairy added—the secret is in adding oil while high-speed blending.) That's when I experienced one of my greatest kitchen nightmares: *I was out of olive oil!* I could have run to the store, but the soup was piping hot and perfect and ready to eat, and frankly, I didn't feel like leaving the house. Then I remembered the mint oil that had stymied me for months. I decided to try it with this soup, and...what a happy accident. The soup was even better than the way I'd been making it before! It still had the same richness I love, but the mint oil added a new fresh taste that surprised me. It was an amazing complement to an already amazing soup.

Of course, if you don't have mint oil, you can certainly make the soup with just extra-virgin olive oil. You could also use lemon oil. I think all versions are fantastic.

By the way, the benefits of broccoli are endless. First and foremost, it is anti-inflammatory and supports your body's natural detoxification process. It contains fiber, which helps aid in digestion, and is an antiaging, immune system builder. It also has powerful antioxidants and is a concentrated source of vitamin C—higher than any other cruciferous vegetable. Although raw broccoli is hard to digest, cooked well and puréed in a soup, it goes down smoothly.

Serves 4

2 tablespoons olive oil

1 small yellow onion, chopped

3 cloves garlic, minced

1 head broccoli, chopped into florets, stem cubed (about 4 cups)

3 cups filtered water

1 teaspoon Himalayan salt

½ teaspoon freshly ground black pepper

2 tablespoons mint oil, plus a little more for garnish

Creamy Broccoli Soup with Mint Oil

In a large stockpot, warm the olive oil over medium heat until it starts to shimmer and easily coats the pan. Add the onion and garlic and cook until translucent, about 5 minutes. Add the broccoli, water, salt, and pepper. Cover and let cook until you can easily put a fork through the broccoli, 12 to 15 minutes.

Remove from the heat and let cool slightly. Carefully pour everything (including the cooking water) into a high-speed blender (you may need to do this in batches). Start blending on a slow setting, working your way up to a faster speed. When on high, start to drizzle a steady stream of the mint oil in

DIY MINT OIL

If you can't find mint oil, you can substitute your favorite flavored oil (like truffle oil or toasted sesame oil). Or, take an extra minute or two and make your own—it's easy. Just pulse a handful of fresh mint with 1 cup olive oil in your blender. Blend and strain (or don't strain if you're feeling rustic) and you have your own homemade mint oil!

through the top. Give it one last blast at high speed, then pour into individual bowls and enjoy. (You could also blend this in the cooking pot with an immersion blender, but you will get a smoother, creamier soup if you use the high-speed blender.)

I like to drizzle a bit of olive oil (or more mint oil) on top of my soup and add some fresh cracked pepper. Simple, clean, yum.

If you have leftovers, you can freeze them for up to 1 month.

AS A KID, I hated cauliflower with a passion. Now it's my most beloved veggie. It's magic. You can make this flowery friend into so many different amazing meals, as you will see in the book: pizza crust (page 103), mashed "potatoes" (page 86), knishes (page 95), and here, a buttery, creamy soup. Loaded with vitamin C, fiber, and so many other wonderful vitamins and minerals, cauliflower can give you the impression that you are eating comforting, filling, starchy food when you're actually being practically puritanical.

This soup is the perfect example of cauliflower magic: It's simple, quick, and tastes like it contains your old friends cream and butter—and yet, it's completely 100 percent dairy free. It's also an adaptable soup. I've made it in many different ways: extremely thick like a gravy, thinner with added "zoodles" (zucchini cut into spaghetti-like strands), or thinner for sipping from a mug. The soup just makes me happy, like I'm getting something very special. It's so rich, you will think you're being sinful, so enjoy the splurge that isn't actually a splurge!

Serves 4

3 tablespoons olive oil, plus more for serving

1 medium yellow onion, chopped

1 large head cauliflower, leaves and stem removed, cut into large chunks

2 teaspoons Himalayan salt

½ teaspoon freshly ground black pepper

1 bay leaf (dried or fresh)

4½ cups filtered water

"Buttery," Creamy Cauliflower Soup

In a large stockpot, heat 1 tablespoon of the olive oil over medium heat until it shimmers and easily coats the pot. Add the onion and sauté until translucent, about 8 minutes. Add the cauliflower, salt, pepper, and bay leaf. Stir to coat everything with the oil and seasonings, then add the water. Cover and cook until the cauliflower is tender enough that you can easily put a fork through it, about 10 minutes. Remove from the heat and let cool slightly.

Remove and discard the bay leaf. Pour everything into a high-speed blender, including the cooking water. Start to blend on slow speed, and gradually increase the speed while adding the remaining 2 tablespoons olive oil, drizzled in a steady stream through the top of the blender. (You could use the immersion blender instead, blending it in the cooking pot.)

When everything is puréed, pour the soup into 4 bowls and drizzle with additional olive oil. Serve warm, at room temperature, or cold.

The soup keeps well for up to 1 month in the freezer—just in case you don't finish every drop.

THIS SOUP was born out of pure need. My body was severely inflamed and I was having a serious autoimmune disease flare. I needed something (anything!) nutritious to get me through this particularly rough patch. I investigated the best ingredients that were anti-inflammatory but also very gentle on the digestion, and this soup was the result. My very aggravated body felt like it had been given a warm blanket. I made a large batch of it and drank it until I felt like me again.

Anti-Inflammatory Mega Soup

Serves 1 or 2

1 tablespoon coconut oil
1 tablespoon olive oil
1 sweet potato, peeled and cubed
1 clove garlic, minced
¼ teaspoon grated fresh ginger
¼ teaspoon ground cloves
¼ teaspoon ground turmeric
¼ teaspoon freshly ground black pepper
Himalayan salt
3 cups filtered water or Bone Broth (page 73)

Heat the coconut oil and olive oil in a large saucepan over medium heat. Add the sweet potato and cook, stirring often, until softened slightly, about 10 minutes. Add the garlic, ginger, cloves, turmeric, pepper, and salt to taste and cook for 2 more minutes. Add the water or bone broth and simmer until the sweet potatoes are completely soft, about 30 minutes. Purée with an immersion blender; or remove from the heat and let cool slightly, then pour into a high-speed blender and blend until smooth. Ladle into a bowl and serve warm. Sip slowly and savor.

THIS SOUP should be on everyone's list of standard winter foods throughout the cold and flu season, when everyone around you is coughing and sneezing. The garlic, ginger, turmeric, and veggies all help boost your immune system so those nasty bugs can't get the best of you. If I'm feeling a little run-down, I'll make a big vat and enjoy soup for two days straight.

The big handfuls of greens in this soup make it just a little bit more challenging to digest, even while making it more immune-boosting. While eating Pure, simply omit the greens or just use half and make sure they are very well-cooked in the soup. Serve steaming hot with Jennifer's Way Classic Artisan Bread (page 213), or Amazing Grain-Free Artisan Bread (page 99) if you are keeping grain free. If you have a cold or congestion, sprinkle more cayenne on top of the soup to help open your sinuses.

Serve 8

Winter Immunity Soup

2 tablespoons olive oil, plus more for serving

4 stalks celery, chopped

3 large carrots, chopped

1 large onion, chopped

3 cloves garlic, minced

1 bay leaf (dried or fresh)

1 teaspoon ground ginger

1/2 teaspoon ground turmeric

2 tablespoons chopped fresh Italian parsley

1 tablespoon chopped fresh thyme

2 tablespoons Himalayan salt, plus more to taste

1 tablespoon freshly ground black pepper, plus more to taste

1/2 teaspoon cayenne pepper

6 1/2 cups filtered water

1 or 2 big handfuls chopped fresh spinach and/or kale

Heat a stockpot or other large pot over medium heat and add the olive oil. Add the celery, carrots, onion, garlic, bay leaf, ginger, and turmeric and sauté for 5 minutes. Add the parsley, thyme, salt, black pepper, cayenne, and water. Bring to a boil, then cover and simmer for 2 to 3 hours, allowing the flavors to develop. Taste and adjust the seasonings as needed. Discard the bay leaf.

Before serving, add the spinach and/or kale. Stir and let cook for another 3 minute for spinach, or another 10 minutes for kale (baby kale only needs about 5 minutes), or until the greens are wilted and soft. Ladle into bowls, drizzle with additional olive oil, and add more salt and black pepper to taste.

Pure Vegetables

Just because you are being extra careful with your digestion doesn't mean you shouldn't be able to actually chew things. Vegetables, in particular, are nutrient dense and extremely valuable in your diet, but raw is off limits. Instead, try these most gentle and soothing versions of vegetable dishes that will make you forget you've given up anything at all.

MASHED POTATOES...sigh...who doesn't *love* them? The problem is, with all the genetically modified white potatoes out there, as well as the nightshade vegetable problem, in addition to the fact that white potatoes practically transform instantly into pure sugar in your body as soon as you swallow them, mashed potatoes can be a problem. Potato lectins can also irritate the immune system. While potatoes are not a staple in my everyday diet, did I want to say good-bye to mashed spuds forever? No, I did not.

Cauliflower to the rescue! I'm in love with the vegetable. Cruciferous vegetables such as cauliflower and broccoli are linked to a significant reduction in the risk of cancers, but cauliflower is also a great source of dietary fiber, which is essential for optimum digestion. It has high amounts of antioxidants and omega-3 fatty acids, which also help prevent chronic inflammation, and it is a potent detoxifier, which can really help you heal.

It is also a chameleon. Cauliflower can be made into almost everything, but I love it most when it stands in for mashed potatoes. (Close second: the Cauliflower Pizza Crust on page 103.) This recipe is so rich and lovely, no one will be able to guess that they are faux—you might even be able to fool your friends into thinking these are actual mashed potatoes.

Serves 4

1 clove garlic, peeled

1 head cauliflower, leaves and stem removed, cut into large chunks

1 tablespoon coconut butter

½ teaspoon Himalayan salt

¼ teaspoon freshly ground black pepper

2 tablespoons olive oil

2 teaspoons chopped fresh rosemary

Mashed Garlic Fauxtatoes

Heat the broiler. Fill a pot with 2 inches of water and add the garlic clove. Place a steamer insert inside the pot. Add the cauliflower to the steamer, cover, and steam for 12 to 15 minutes, until very tender when pierced with a fork.

Transfer the cauliflower, garlic, and 1 tablespoon of the garlic water to a high-speed blender or food processor and add the coconut butter, salt, and pepper. Purée until smooth, adding 1 tablespoon of the olive oil in a slow stream while mixing.

Transfer the cauliflower mixture to an ovenproof dish and broil to make a very lightly crusty top. Watch it closely, as this will happen fast—probably in less than 5 minutes, depending on your broiler.

Garnish with fresh rosemary and drizzle with the remaining 1 tablespoon olive oil.

GROWING UP, I had no idea what a parsnip was. Now that I have been officially introduced to this underused vegetable that looks like a fat white carrot, I know that it is full of vitamins and minerals, fiber and potassium, and vitamin C (not unlike the potato). Adding parsnips to your cauliflower mash adds a velvety texture and a slightly different, mysterious, and pleasant flavor. And of course, the result is once again a lot like mashed potatoes—any time I can re-create a texture and a taste of my childhood, but do it in a better way for my body, I'm thrilled.

Cauliflower and Parsnip Mash

Serves 4 to 6

1 large head cauliflower, leaves and stem removed, cut into large chunks

1½ large parsnips, peeled and chopped

2 tablespoons Homemade Hemp Milk (page 144) or other nondairy milk of your choice

1½ tablespoons coconut oil or olive oil

1 tablespoon coconut butter, ghee, or other nondairy butter of choice

1 teaspoon Himalayan salt

Dash of freshly ground black pepper

Fill a pot with 2 inches of water and place a steamer insert inside the pot. Add the cauliflower and parsnips to the steamer, cover, and steam for 12 to 15 minutes, until the vegetables are very tender when pierced with a fork.

Transfer the vegetables to a large mixing bowl. Add the remaining ingredients and whip with a hand mixer (or in a stand mixer) until creamy. Serve hot.

I PUT THIS RECIPE in the Pure section, but frankly, it belongs anywhere and everywhere because I eat it constantly—for special occasions, for every day, for meals, for snacks—it is that delicious and versatile and soothing too. In fact, I don't just eat sweet potatoes whipped—I also eat them mashed, smashed, baked, made into fries, or fancied-up for the holidays with maple syrup and gluten-free marshmallows, then under the broiler for a melty crispy topping (page 261)—so good. I mean, *so* good, *to-die-for* good. But this recipe is still my favorite way to eat them, especially when I am keeping things simple and eating Pure. This recipe is calming, soothing, and mood enhancing. And even though this and other sweet potato recipes taste decadent, they are nutrient dense, loaded with vitamin A, vitamin C, and vitamin B_6. They are also a lifesaver when you are not eating grains as they can satiate that starchy craving you may be chasing. Breakfast, lunch, dinner, whatever!

My point is: *Eat this often!*

Whipped Sweet Potatoes

Serves 4 to 6

2 large sweet potatoes, peeled and cubed

1 tablespoon raw honey

1 teaspoon kosher salt

½ teaspoon ground cinnamon

5 tablespoons olive oil

Fill a large stockpot with water, add the sweet potatoes, and bring to a boil. Reduce the heat and simmer until a fork can go through the potatoes easily, about 15 to 20 minutes, depending on how big the cubes are.

Drain, transfer to a mixing bowl, and add the honey, salt, cinnamon, and 3 tablespoons of the olive oil. Whip with a hand mixer (or in a stand mixer) until smooth, drizzling in the remaining 2 tablespoons olive oil as you go.

IT MAY SOUND CRAZY, but one of my favorite things to do is food shopping. I love walking through the farmers' markets in Brooklyn and thinking of all the possibilities. To me, this is as exciting as any adventure. The pride small farmers take in their fruits and vegetables is so personal and so moving. When you're shopping at your farmers' market, take a moment to ask questions. You might make a new friend, and also get to hear how those beautiful squashes or tomatoes or root vegetables got that way. Then it's your turn to transform them into something delicious.

I felt like I was celebrating the late-summer harvest in the best possible way when I found beautiful squashes, carrots, and parsnips at my local farmers' market, and roasted them. Sometimes I have this recipe as a side dish and sometimes as a dessert, or even a snack. It will keep in the refrigerator for about 2 days.

Serves 8

2 acorn or butternut squashes

5 or 6 yellow and orange carrots

3 or 4 parsnips

¼ cup olive oil

1 teaspoon real maple syrup

½ teaspoon ground cinnamon

½ teaspoon Himalayan salt

Roasted Autumn Squash and Root Vegetables

Preheat the oven to 400°F. Peel and chop all the vegetables into bite-size pieces and place in a large bowl. In a separate small bowl, combine the olive oil, maple syrup, cinnamon, and salt. Whisk to combine, then pour over the veggies. Stir, making sure all of the pieces are well coated.

Spread the vegetables on a baking sheet and bake until tender (when you can put a fork through easily), 45 minutes to 1 hour. Serve hot.

SPAGHETTI SQUASH is the answer to a pasta lover's prayers. The simple gourd can make dinner feel special, without much effort—all you have to do is run a fork through the halved squash after baking, and you've got tasty, pasta-like strands that can quench your craving for pasta—but with a fraction of the starch and none of the grains. You can literally sauce spaghetti squash 50 different ways—the most popular probably being with a traditional Bolognese sauce (page 256). Here, I've paired the beautiful squash with the no-fail combo of garlic and olive oil. It's a great recipe for the whole family, but if you have a crowd, make a lot—especially if you invite me. I've been known to eat the entire squash myself.

Serves 4

1 spaghetti squash
2 tablespoons plus ½ cup olive oil
3 cloves garlic, minced
1 teaspoon red pepper flakes
Juice of ½ lemon
2 cups fresh spinach
1 tablespoon sesame seeds (optional)

Spaghetti Squash with Garlic and Oil

Note: It is extremely difficult and even dangerous to cut a spaghetti squash in half, even with a sharp knife, because the skin is so hard. See the first step for a much easier and safer way to halve your spaghetti squash.

Preheat the oven to 375°F.

Using the tip of a sharp knife, poke holes, about an inch apart, all around the squash where you want to cut it in half. Put the whole squash in the microwave and cook on high for 5 minutes. Remove it and you will discover it is much easier to cut in half. Using a spoon, scoop out the seeds.

Rub each half all over with 1 tablespoon of the olive oil and place cut-side down in a shallow baking pan. Roast for 30 minutes, then flip cut-side up. Roast for 10 more minutes, until a fork goes into the flesh easily.

Let the squash sit for a few minutes, until cool enough to handle. Using a fork, scrape out the squash, which will come out in spaghetti-like strands.

Heat the remaining ½ cup olive oil in a large skillet over medium heat. Add the garlic, red pepper flakes, and lemon juice, stirring once after each addition. Add the spaghetti squash and toss until coated. Serve hot over fresh spinach. If they don't bother you, you can sprinkle the whole thing with sesame seeds, but if you are being strictly Pure, leave those out.

WHILE ON a much-needed vacation with my dear friend Rick, he made incredible guacamole every day, while the rest of us sat on the beach being lazy. I brought along my Pure biscuits (page 69), and we all used them to scrape that guacamole bowl clean. Avocado, as you may already know, is one of the best sources of healthy fat. Pair that with sitting on the beach with good friends, and I can't think of a better prescription for feeling well.

When I'm feeling up for raw vegetables, I might dip carrots and celery in this. It's a great topping for grain-free bread or toast and—call me a rebel—I've even been known to plop some on my baked sweet potato. I've changed this slightly from Rick's original masterpiece, but the spirit is still there and this is by far the best guacamole I've ever had anywhere—thanks in part to the secret power ingredient and our old friend: turmeric!

Rick's Guacamole

Serves 4 to 8

2 ripe avocados

1 red onion, diced

2 tablespoons olive oil

1 teaspoon paprika

1 teaspoon ground turmeric

1 teaspoon fresh lime juice

1 teaspoon fresh lemon juice

½ teaspoon Himalayan salt, plus more to taste

Handful of chopped fresh cilantro and/or Italian parsley

Mash everything together in a bowl. You could use a mortar and pestle, which I really love because it presses everything together and seems to bring out the flavor more. Or, just mash it with a fork. I also like to drizzle a little more olive oil over the top as well, because you can't have too much good fat. Consume joyfully.

If on the off chance you have leftovers, store them with an avocado pit, drizzle with a little more lemon juice, and press wax paper, parchment paper, or plastic wrap on the guac so it touches as much of the surface as possible. You can keep it for 1 day this way. Longer than that and, sadly, guacamole turns brown. However, I advise you to eat it all because it's never as good it is when it's freshly made.

TO ME, this is a quintessential Italian dish. When I was a kid, we didn't get together with our extended family very often, as everyone was spread out and had busy schedules. When we did, though, I was in heaven because I would finally get to see my long-lost cousins. When we gathered, the whole huge extended family would end up at some authentic Italian restaurant. I remember all us kids running around the restaurant, probably tormenting all the other customers. But as soon as the food came, I got very serious. (Even then, I was all about the food.)

I especially remember the zucchini fries at those Italian restaurants. We never made them at home, so it was a special treat, and the most amazing thing about them was that they were both delicious and *a vegetable!* As a kid, this blew my mind

As an adult, I missed them and decided it was time to remake my old love in a cleaner, healthier way. So I give you zucchini sticks, fried in coconut oil so you can make the oil really hot to get a nice brown, crunchy outside. (You don't want to do this with olive oil, another super-healthy oil, because it degrades if it gets too hot.) You and your little ones can make these and enjoy them with glee!

Serves 8

¾ cup cassava flour

1 teaspoon Himalayan salt, plus more to taste

¼ teaspoon freshly ground black pepper, plus more to taste

Pinch of garlic powder

½ cup coconut milk (or nondairy milk of choice)

1 to 2 cups coconut oil, for frying (less if you have a small, deep pan)

4 medium zucchini, peeled and cut into ¼-inch-thick fry-shaped pieces

Fried Zucchini Sticks

In a large bowl, combine the cassava flour, salt, pepper, and garlic powder. In a separate bowl, place the coconut milk.

Add 1 inch of coconut oil to a heavy-bottom skillet—enough to be able to submerge the zucchini fries. Heat the oil over medium-high heat until melted and hot enough that a bit of water sizzles when dropped in.

Carefully dip your zucchini sticks in the coconut milk, then dredge them in the flour mixture, shaking off any excess. Add in batches to the hot oil (you should not have more than one layer at a time) and fry for 3 minutes, or until the fries are golden-brown. Pull them out with a slotted spoon and drain on several layers of paper towels. Sprinkle with salt and pepper to taste.

KNISHES, oh how I loved you. Yes, past tense. I never thought they could reappear in my life, but then I met the almighty cauliflower. If this cookbook inspires you to do just one thing, it should be to buy a head of cauliflower and discover that you can transform it into something amazing.

I played many sports as a kid, when I wasn't sick with my stomach issues (thanks to my undiagnosed celiac disease). But the sport that brought knishes into my life was softball. Throughout the entire game, I would think about buying one at a nearby deli that made the best knishes I had ever tasted, and after the game was over, that was the first place I would go. Maybe that's why I was benched so many times! I was focusing on knishes instead of the game. Oh well, those first few bites of my after-game knish made me feel so good, I didn't mind at all. Little did I know that the knishes contributed to my ill feelings later in the day, and in general, just added to the gluten load I didn't realize was harming me. Fortunately, this version is Pure and soothing and won't harm your digestion one bit.

Serve with mustard. If you are eating in the Clean category, you could also dip them in marinara sauce.

Serves 8

1 head cauliflower, leaves and stem removed, cut or broken into bite-size pieces

2 tablespoons cassava flour

2 tablespoons unsweetened applesauce (or, if you tolerate them, 1 teaspoon chia seeds mixed with 2 teaspoons water and 1 tablespoon unsweetened applesauce)

1 teaspoon dried onion flakes

½ teaspoon garlic salt

½ teaspoon Himalayan salt, plus more for sprinkling

Mustard, for serving (optional)

Jen's Cauliflower Knishes

Preheat the oven to 400°F. Place the cauliflower in a food processor and pulse until it resembles rice. Transfer to a large saucepan and cover with water. Bring to a boil, lower the heat to medium, and cook until the cauliflower is tender, 5 to 7 minutes.

Drain the cauliflower in a strainer lined with cheesecloth, then run cool water over the cauliflower. Using the cheesecloth, squeeze the excess water from the cauliflower.

In a large bowl, combine the cooked cauliflower with the cassava flour, applesauce, onion flakes, garlic salt, and Himalayan salt. Using your hands, form small, nugget-like shapes with the mixture and place on a baking sheet. Sprinkle with additional Himalayan salt.

Bake, flipping the nuggets once, for 25 minutes, until they have turned golden-brown. Remove from the oven and turn the broiler to high. Place them back under the broiler for 5 minutes to brown the tops. Serve hot, either plain or with mustard for dipping.

THIS IS one of the simplest recipes in this book, celebrating the beautiful creature that is the artichoke. Not all good things in life need to be hard. Not feeling up to cooking? Here's your answer: Artichokes, garlic, olive oil, lemon, and salt—what could be better? I simply steam the artichokes and then pour the garlic water over them for extra flavor. Artichokes are more than a pretty face. They are also packed with fiber and iron.

I make this recipe an entire meal by serving with a freshly made, crunchy loaf of bread for dipping in the leftover broth (like the one on page 99). Although I don't recommend drinking alcohol when you are eating Pure, I have been known, on special occasions, to pair the artichokes and bread with a bold red wine, when I am feeling up to it. Put on some Frank Sinatra and you will swear you are in Italy (or at my house).

Serves 4

4 artichokes

2 cloves garlic, peeled and minced

¼ cup olive oil, plus more for serving

Juice of ½ lemon

Himalayan salt

Freshly ground black pepper

Steamed Lemon– Garlic Artichokes

Clean the artichokes by cutting off the pointy tips and bottom stem. Cut so that the artichokes stand upright.

Fill a large saucepan with about 1 inch of water and place the artichokes in a steamer tray (or directly in the water is also fine). Place the garlic around the artichokes and drizzle the olive oil over everything. Squeeze the lemon over the top and sprinkle generously with salt and pepper. Cover and steam over medium heat until a leaf comes off easily, about 30 minutes.

Transfer to a platter to serve. You can pour the remaining steaming water over the artichokes, then drizzle with olive oil and more salt and pepper to taste.

And, in case you've never eaten artichokes before and are staring at this gorgeous dish wondering what to do, just pull off the tender leaves one at a time. Draw your teeth over the meaty part to scrape it off and devour it, then discard the stripped leaf. It's like heaven on a plate.

Pure Breads and Crusts

Being off grains for a while (or permanently) doesn't mean you have to be off delicious, warm, comforting baked treats like biscuits, bread, pie, and pizza. Trust me: Baking without grains is an art, and it's not an easy one to master. I've experimented a lot in this area (read: *for years*), and these are my purest, gentlest, and hard-won anti-inflammatory baked creations. Prepare to have your mind blown.

THIS IS THE HOLY GRAIL. Grain-free bread! Real, honest-to-goodness, crusty, doughy bread. I make this bread and eat it *all day and night!* It keeps me sane and away from grains my body can't handle. This is different from my Classic Artisan Bread (page 213) in the Indulgent section because it does not contain any grains. Yes, this tasty loaf is grain free, and yet...*it is bread!* Even grain-eaters and gluten-eaters (and everyone I've ever served this bread to) can't tell the difference between this loaf and simple, good bread. This particular recipe took me two years to perfect, and it was worth every second.

I use the bread for everything, from bread crumbs and croutons to my Banana-Soaked French Toast (page 154) for a real treat that is still Pure. Yes, you *can have French toast!* And let's not forget the almighty *sandwich!* There are a few wonderful sandwich recipes in this book (pages 171, 239, 240)—and with this bread, you can have them all and still stay Pure and grain free. The bread is like a free pass, a golden ticket, the winning lottery numbers! Grain-free, gluten-free, dairy-free, soy-free, corn-free, nut-free bread? Yup! As you can see, I get very excited about this bread, but I think you will be too when you try it.

Note that the recipe does contain chia seeds. They are soaked in water and turn into a nice gel that helps hold the bread together, but if you are strictly anti-seed right now, you may want to wait to make the bread until you are feeling a little stronger. I put it in the Pure category because, for me, knowing that I can have a simple piece of satisfying bread keeps me on the Pure straight-and-narrow. I want to heal but I also want to live, and this bread makes that possible for me. Only you can decide if the chia seed element is a deal-breaker for you right now.

Makes two 6-inch round loaves

1 cup cassava flour
¼ cup coconut flour
¼ cup plantain flour
1 cup tapioca starch
¾ cup arrowroot starch
2 teaspoons baking soda
1 tablespoon xanthan gum
1 tablespoon Himalayan salt
1¼ cups warm water
¼ cup olive oil
1 tablespoon raw honey
1 tablespoon dry yeast
¼ cup chia seeds mixed with
   ¾ cup warm water
1 tablespoon apple cider vinegar
Fresh rosemary (optional)
Kosher salt (optional)

Amazing Grain-Free Artisan Bread

In a stand mixer with the paddle attachment, mix the cassava flour, coconut flour, plantain flour, tapioca starch, arrowroot starch, 1 teaspoon of the baking soda, the xanthan gum, and the Himalayan salt until just combined.

In a small bowl, combine the warm water, olive oil, honey, and yeast. Set aside for 5 minutes to allow the yeast to activate.

Add the yeast mixture and chia seed mixture to the dry ingredients in the mixer bowl and mix on medium speed until just combined. In another small bowl, combine the remaining 1 teaspoon baking soda and the vinegar and add to the dough

⟶ recipe continues

(it will be fizzy). Turn the mixer to high speed and whip for an additional 2 to 3 minutes, until everything is well incorporated.

Put the dough in a glass or plastic container with a loose-fitting lid, and let it sit in a warm dry place for about 1 hour, until doubled in size.

Preheat the oven to 400°F. Line a baking sheet with parchment paper.

Get your hands wet, then scoop out about half the dough (it should be about the size of a grapefruit). Form it into a ball, and place it on the parchment paper. Wet your hands again and smooth out the top of the dough, flattening it down a little into a round loaf shape, then score an X into the top with a sharp knife. You can leave it plain, or sprinkle the top with rosemary (or your favorite herb) and kosher salt. Repeat with the remaining dough. Both loaves should fit on a large baking sheet.

Bake for 45 to 55 minutes, until the bread has reached an internal temperature of 210°F (use your meat thermometer for this). Cool completely, as the bread will continue to bake for a while. After the bread is completely cool, slice it. Serve, or store the slices in a paper bag and leave on the counter for easy use for up to 4 days; or freeze in an airtight plastic bag for up to 1 month.

THERE IS something homey and comforting about pie that makes me very happy, especially when I use this piecrust. It's a lifesaver when I have to be grain free, because this crust (unlike the other piecrust in this book) is 100 percent in line with Pure eating. Seriously, I will make a fruit pie or a pumpkin pie and eat it for breakfast. It satiates that starchy craving and that sweet craving without adding much starch or sweetness.

I have filled it with many different things, but some of my favorites are fresh blueberries, pears (page 135), or Raw Cacao Pudding (page 67). You can also eliminate the sweetener to make a savory crust and fill with roasted butternut squash mixed with sage (page 175), or sliced cooked sweet potatoes and zucchini for a delicious vegetable tart. You can also use the dough for hand pies (page 117).

Makes 1 crust

- ¾ cup palm shortening, nondairy butter (such as Earth Balance), or coconut oil
- ½ cup coconut flour
- ¼ cup cassava flour
- ¾ cup arrowroot starch
- 1 tablespoon maple sugar or date sugar (optional)
- ½ teaspoon ground cinnamon
- ¼ teaspoon Himalayan salt
- ½ teaspoon ground vanilla bean (or 1 teaspoon gluten-free vanilla extract)
- ⅓ cup cold water

Grain-Free Piecrust

Refrigerate the shortening, butter, or coconut oil for at least 20 minutes, until well chilled.

In a large bowl, combine the coconut flour, cassava flour, and arrowroot starch with a fork or whisk. (Really sift through it all to get out any lumps.) Add the sugar (if using), cinnamon, salt, and vanilla and mix again. Cut the cold shortening into dice-size cubes and add to the flour mixture along with the cold water, and mix until a dough forms. You can do this with a fork, or use a food processor to process quickly, until the mixture resembles large crumbs.

Once everything is combined, gather up the dough into a ball and wrap with plastic wrap. Refrigerate for 15 minutes.

If you are accustomed to piecrust dough that you roll out, know that this is not like that. This dough is better for pressing into the pie pan. Get your hands wet and work the dough into a smooth shape. Put it in an 8- or 9-inch pie or tart pan and press down to cover the bottom and sides. Keep wetting your hands and working it. There are no mistakes here. Just get it in there as well as you can and it will taste great.

To pre-bake this crust for pre-cooked or raw fillings, bake for 12 minutes at 350°F. This crust won't brown, but it will still be pre-baked.

YOU WILL not believe how well my friend Mr. Cauliflower transforms into *pizza*. Yes, a *crunchy* cauliflower pizza crust! I've made this for gluten-eating friends, and they *loved* it. The secret to the crust is squeezing the water from the cauliflower completely after cooking it.

You could make this with tomato sauce just like a regular pizza crust, but if you are completely eliminating nightshades from your diet while eating Pure, try it with arugula and pear drizzled with olive oil and sprinkled with Himalayan salt. Or opt for sautéed spinach with garlic and some butternut squash. All are delicious. And see the box (page 106) for more ideas. You can even just make the crust, sprinkle it with olive oil and Himalayan salt, and eat it as a bread. You've got options.

Cauliflower Pizza Crust

Makes 1 medium crust, serving 6

1 large head cauliflower, leaves and stem removed

½ cup cassava flour

1 teaspoon dried parsley

½ teaspoon garlic powder

½ teaspoon dried onion flakes

1 teaspoon Himalayan salt

¼ cup unsweetened applesauce (or use 3 tablespoons chia seeds mixed with 6 tablespoons warm water, if you are eating from the Clean section of this book)

Toppings of choice (see box, page 106)

Preheat the oven to 400°F. Line a baking sheet with parchment paper.

Using a cheese or box grater, grate the cauliflower by hand, or put it in a food processor and pulse until the cauliflower is pea-size. Don't over-grate or mince—you want good-size shreds. Place the shreds in a saucepan and cover with water. Cover, bring to a simmer, and cook for 5 to 7 minutes. Drain and transfer to a bowl to sit until cool enough to handle (you can cool it in the refrigerator for a minute or two to help).

Place the cauliflower in a clean dishtowel or paper towels and wring to squeeze out all the water. This takes some time. You may need to use quite a few paper towels, but the more water

→ recipe continues

The pizza pictured is topped with crushed tomatoes and basil, which is great if you are eating from the Clean section of this book, because tomatoes are a nightshade. If you are eating strictly Pure, opt for non-night-shade vegetables, as suggested in the recipe. I like fresh rosemary, sea salt, and olive oil, or fresh figs and arugula.

Cauliflower Pizza Crust,
continued

PIZZA TOPPINGS

Grain-free pizza crusts can be a
bit less sturdy than regular pizza
crusts, so it's a good idea to keep
the toppings light. Some ideas:
fresh figs, olives, pear slices,
spinach, garlic slices, fresh basil.
Grill vegetables before using
them as toppings so they don't
release water into the crust.
Or keep it light, with simple
toppings like a drizzle of olive oil
and a topping of rosemary and
kosher salt, or sliced olives and
sautéed mushrooms, or thinly
sliced tomatoes and fresh torn
basil leaves.

you get out, the crunchier your crust will be. When you've
gotten out as much water as possible, return the cauliflower
to the bowl and add the cassava flour, parsley, garlic powder,
onion flakes, and salt and stir with a wooden spoon. Add the
applesauce (or chia mixture) and mix again.

Take your cauliflower "dough" and press it onto the lined baking
sheet, using the palms of your hands to flatten and press the
dough outward to form a thin (but not too thin) crust—maybe
½ inch thick. (For an even more authentic crust, bake on a pizza
stone: Place the parchment paper on a cutting board. Shape the
dough into approximately a large grapefruit size on the paper,
then carefully transfer the dough to a baking stone that you have
been preheating in the oven.)

Bake for 25 minutes, then flip carefully using a spatula (or two)
and bake for another 10 minutes, until firm. Remove from the
oven and top to your heart's delight with toppings (but not too
heavy, so the crust doesn't weaken and break). Bake for another
5 minutes with the toppings, until they are warmed through, if
you want the toppings warm.

PLANTAINS—those savory, starchy fruits that look like big bananas—have become another sneaky starch that is appearing more often in health food markets these days as an alternative flour. It also happens to make an excellent pizza base! Plantains are super versatile—they can be made into waffles, muffins, and cookies (see my recipe for chocolate chip cookies made with plantains on page 121). But if you've got a pizza itch to scratch and you've never tried plantains, let this be your first plantain experiment. Your health and your family's well-being is worth trying something new! It really is simple to do, so don't get scared off by a new ingredient. It just takes a few steps; take your time and see what happens. I promise you will be happy you did. You can top the crust with anything your heart desires, whether you are eating Pure, Clean, or Indulgent. For topping ideas, see the box on page 106.

Makes 1 medium crust, serving 6

⅓ cup olive oil

½ cup water

2 cups cubed peeled green plantains (not the black sweet ones—look for the green ones, which are savory), from about 2 large plantains

1 cup cassava flour

1 cup arrowroot starch

1 teaspoon garlic powder

1 teaspoon onion flakes

1 teaspoon dried parsley

Toppings of choice (see the box on page 106 for some ideas)

Plantain Pizza Crust

Preheat the oven to 400°F. Line a baking sheet with parchment paper.

In a high-speed blender, combine the olive oil and water first, then the plantains, flour, starch, garlic powder, onion flakes, and parsley. Start on slow speed and gradually work the ingredients together, eventually increasing to high speed until a dough-like consistency forms.

Transfer the dough to the lined baking sheet and press out a round or square shape, about ¼ inch thick. Bake for 20 minutes. Flip the crust using a spatula (or two), and bake for another 5 minutes, until the crust feels firm.

Remove from the oven and add your toppings of choice. Bake for another 5 minutes, until the toppings are warmed through, if desired. Or, if you want to really brown the toppings, put them under the broiler for 5 minutes.

Pure Meals

For some people, meat is sometimes difficult to digest, and when I am eating Pure, I'm not about to have prime rib or a T-bone. However, meat gives you more easily digested protein than plants. Certainly for me, roasted chicken or baked salmon is a lot easier to digest than beans and rice. Here are my favorite meat dishes for when I am eating Pure, and while I would never force anyone to eat meat if they are against it, I do believe the recipes are potently nourishing as well as savory and delicious.

THIS SIMPLE RECIPE is a weekly favorite. It's a quick, one-pan dinner, perfect for midweek when you're pressed for time but still need something substantial. If your diet includes some grains I suggest making Italian Bread Crumbs (page 216) and sprinkling them on top of the chicken and asparagus for extra crunch.

One-Dish Chicken with Asparagus

Serves 4

4 bone-in chicken breasts (preferably organic), sliced in half lengthwise

Drizzle of olive oil

1 lemon, halved

1 teaspoon ground turmeric

1 teaspoon Himalayan salt

½ teaspoon freshly ground black pepper

1 bunch asparagus, woody ends trimmed

Preheat the oven to 350°F.

Place the chicken breasts in a large baking dish and drizzle with olive oil and the juice of one lemon half. Sprinkle with the turmeric, ½ teaspoon of the salt, and ¼ teaspoon of the pepper. Place the asparagus around the chicken and drizzle with more olive oil and the juice from the other lemon half. Season with the remaining salt and pepper. Bake for about 25 minutes, until you can put a fork through the asparagus easily. Insert a meat thermometer into the chicken breast; it should register 165°F when cooked. Serve warm and enjoy immediately.

THIS CHICKEN is a showstopper. I have made roasted chicken for holidays, for slow lazy Sundays with friends, and even dinner parties (by doubling the recipe). It is a second-to-none centerpiece on a lovely set table that tastes even better than it looks. Serve it with sweet potatoes, any non-potato mash recipe in Pure Vegetables (page 85), or white potatoes, if you are eating Clean.

A major bonus to this recipe is that you end up with a chicken carcass that you can use to make bone broth...*for free!* So, save that carcass, pick off any remaining meat, and start the bone broth in your slow cooker after dinner (recipe on page 73). Roast chicken is the meal that keeps on giving.

Serves 4 (with leftover chicken)

Roasted Lemon-Herb Chicken with Root Vegetables

1 whole organic chicken, 3 to 5 pounds
4½ cups cubed peeled root vegetables (any combination of carrots, beets, butternut squash, sweet potatoes, parsnips, and/or Brussels sprouts will work)
¼ cup olive oil
1 lemon, juiced, rind reserved
2 tablespoons raw honey

3 cloves garlic, 1 peeled and minced, the other 2 peeled but left whole
2 tablespoons chopped fresh Italian parsley
1 tablespoon chopped fresh rosemary
1 tablespoon fresh thyme
Himalayan salt
Freshly ground black pepper

Preheat the oven to 475°F. Rinse the chicken with cold water and pat dry with paper towels. Place in a wire rack in a roasting pan and set aside.

Place the cubed vegetables in a large bowl. In a separate bowl, combine the olive oil, lemon juice, honey, minced garlic, parsley, rosemary, thyme, ½ teaspoon salt, and ½ teaspoon pepper. Whisk together and pour about one-fourth over the vegetables. Mix until the vegetables are coated.

Pour the remaining mixture over the chicken and rub it in with your hands. Place the lemon rind into the cavity of the chicken, along with the 2 whole garlic cloves. Arrange the root vegetables in the pan around the chicken. Sprinkle everything with more salt and pepper. Roast for 25 minutes. Reduce the heat to 400°F and roast for an additional 45 minutes, until a meat thermometer inserted into the thickest part of the thigh registers 165°F.

Place the chicken on a cutting board or platter, cover with a tea towel or a tent of parchment paper or foil, and let rest for 15 minutes. Serve the vegetables alongside the chicken, carving it at the table.

THIS IS my favorite go-to dish for dinner, no matter how I'm feeling. It's easy, but doesn't look it. If you're hosting a dinner party or even a date for two, salmon in parchment is a true people-pleaser. It gives off a fancy vibe (but isn't) and makes you feel like you've had a meal that was truly made with love. The recipe as written serves one, so it's great for just yourself, but you can also make as many of the packets as you like—simply scale up the ingredients according to how many people you need to feed. Everyone will love opening up their parchment packet to reveal a delicious dinner.

You can replace the veggies and herbs suggested here with your favorites, or the ones that are seasonal (colored tomatoes and summer squashes are nice for summer, but tomatoes are nightshade vegetables, so avoid them for Pure eating). In this recipe I use mushrooms and spinach, which are hearty and warming in colder weather. You can also use another fish if salmon isn't to your taste, but use a similarly firm-fleshed fish like halibut or cod. This dish is packed with goodness, great fats, and protein and is always in my weekly meal plan.

Serves 1

1 fillet wild-caught salmon (or any firm, white, flaky fish), typically 4 to 6 ounces, but use whatever size piece you want to eat

1 small zucchini, peeled, if vegetable skins bother your digestion, and sliced

1 small handful fresh spinach

1 medium portobello mushroom (not the big cap), chopped (or about ¼ cup chopped mushrooms)

2 tablespoons fresh lemon juice

2 tablespoons olive oil or sesame oil

1 tablespoon sesame seeds (optional—only if you can handle seeds)

½ teaspoon ground ginger

½ teaspoon ground turmeric

Himalayan salt

Freshly ground black pepper

Baked Wild Salmon in Parchment

Preheat the oven to 375°F. Cut a piece of parchment paper about 12 inches square.

Place the fish in the middle of the parchment and top with the vegetables. Drizzle everything with the lemon juice and oil, then sprinkle with the sesame seeds (if using), ginger, and turmeric. Wrap everything up into a tight package by folding the edge nearest you over the fish, then folding the opposite edge over that. Finally, fold each side underneath the fish.

Bake for about 20 minutes. Carefully unwrap the parchment and test to see if the fish flakes or breaks apart easily. If it still looks raw you can bake the packet for another 5 minutes. Season with salt and pepper and dig in!

VARIATION I also love to make a Mediterranean version of this recipe, with lemon slices, summer squashes, chopped fresh basil, and cherry tomatoes (reserve tomatoes for Clean eating).

I DON'T REMEMBER eating a lot of tuna steak growing up in Brooklyn. It was something that seemed a bit fancy for us, and for some reason we never had it. A tuna fish sandwich was more the norm; little chunks of fish that came out of a can is what I knew. I first had a real tuna steak when I was around 18, waiting tables in Manhattan trying to earn enough money to pay for my acting classes. As the waitstaff, we had to try all the new specials to be able to explain them to the customers. I remember seeing the tuna, sitting on the plate looking almost like a piece of steak. When broken open, it was bright pink inside. That was such a surprise to me—it was nothing like the tuna sandwiches I had as a kid, that was for sure! But boy, did it taste good.

I still think a good piece of freshly caught tuna is simply amazing—rich in protein and seemingly gourmet, even though it is very easy to cook. Just purchase the tuna from a reputable fishmonger and make sure to not overcook it. I also don't eat tuna more than once every week or two, because it can contain mercury, which isn't good for anyone. Serve with Mashed Garlic Fauxtatoes (page 86) for a delicious meal.

Serves 4

1/3 cup olive oil, plus 1 tablespoon for the pan
Juice of 1 lemon
1 teaspoon raw honey
1/4 cup chopped fresh Italian parsley
1 tablespoon chopped fresh chives
1/2 teaspoon Himalayan salt
1/2 teaspoon freshly ground black pepper
4 tuna steaks, approximately 6 ounces each

Herb-Lemon-Honey Tuna Steaks

In a small bowl, combine the olive oil, lemon juice, honey, parsley, chives, salt, and pepper and whisk together. Transfer to a large ziplock bag, place the tuna steaks inside, and fully coat with the mixture. Seal and refrigerate for 30 minutes.

Heat a cast-iron pan over high heat. Add the tablespoon of olive oil and when the pan is very hot, just starting to smoke, add the tuna steaks and sear for 2 to 3½ minutes on each side. The center should still be red, or reddish-pink for a more well-done fish. Don't allow the fish to lose the pink, or it will become too tough. Transfer to a plate and let rest for 5 minutes before slicing and serving warm.

YES, it's a whole fish, and yes, it looks intimidating. But trust me, it's not. I thought the same thing once, but all you need is a fishmonger who will clean the fish for you, and you're ready to go. I bought branzino at my local Whole Foods, and they were wonderful about scaling, gutting, and cleaning it for me, no problem.

I first had branzino (it's also called European sea bass) at a restaurant and found it to be a lifesaver because even if the pan or grill is contaminated, the insides of the whole fish stay clean, and that's awesome. If ordering at a restaurant, just be sure to ask about what they put inside the fish, but usually it's pretty much what is in this recipe. It's truly a *wow* dinner, and much simpler to make than it looks. I pair it with sweet potatoes and spinach for a great meal. Watch for the bones when you are eating the fish.

Serves 2

1 lemon

3 cloves garlic, peeled

2 whole branzino (1 to 1½ pounds each), scaled, gutted, and cleaned

Himalayan salt

Olive oil

2 sprigs fresh rosemary, plus 1 teaspoon chopped

1 handful fresh Italian parsley

¼ cup dry white wine

2 sweet potatoes, peeled and cut into ¼-inch-thick fries

3 handfuls fresh spinach

Whole Baked Branzino over Spinach with Rosemary Sweet Potato Fries

Set the oven racks in the middle and bottom positions. Preheat the oven to 425°F. Line a baking sheet with parchment paper. Cut 4 thin slices from the lemon and reserve both the slices and the remaining lemon. Thinly slice 2 of the garlic cloves.

Place the fish in a baking dish. Season both sides of the fish with salt, drizzle with ¼ cup olive oil, and rub to coat. Stuff each of the fish cavities with 2 lemon slices, half the sliced garlic, 1 rosemary sprig, and half the parsley, then season with salt. Pour the wine over the fish and into the pan. Add the remaining garlic clove to the pan and squeeze the lemon over the fish.

In a medium bowl, combine the sweet potato fries, 2 tablespoons olive oil, the chopped rosemary, and salt to taste. Spread out on the lined baking sheet and place on the bottom rack of the oven. Place the fish on the middle rack. Roast for 20 minutes, until the fish flakes with a fork and the sweet potatoes are fork-tender.

On a large serving platter, toss the spinach with a drizzle of olive oil and sprinkle with salt. Place the fish over the bed of spinach, and pour half the liquid from the pan over it. Serve with the sweet potatoes on the side.

SOMETHING I LIKE TO DO with piecrust, either grain free or gluten free, is to make hand pies. Hand pies are so much fun to make for a crowd, and kids in particular think it's fun to make and eat them. Pass them around at a party, or make them for holidays with seasonal fillings (like dark chocolate or pumpkin on Halloween, leftover turkey and gravy after Thanksgiving, or baby vegetables and sweet potatoes, or fresh strawberries with mint sprigs in the spring). Your only limit is your creativity. I've tried these lots of different ways, and they are always incredibly delicious.

At first you may think hand pies are difficult to make, but the more you work with the dough, the more you will get used to how the dough responds and what works and tastes best—hand pies are an art form so don't worry if they don't look perfect the first few times. They will still taste great.

Hand Pies

Makes 4 hand pies, but this recipe can be doubled, tripled, and so on, for larger groups

1 recipe Old-Fashioned Gluten-Free Piecrust (page 205) or Grain-Free Piecrust* (page 102) (omit added sweetener for savory recipes)

½ cup (or a little more) of your favorite savory or sweet filling**

Divide the dough into 4 pieces and press out into approximately 6-inch rounds on a baking sheet. They don't have to be perfect. Spoon 2 to 3 tablespoons of filling on one side of each round, fold the dough over, and pinch the edges together. Or make 8 (3-inch) rounds, put 2 tablespoons of filling on 4 of the rounds, cover with the other 4 rounds, and pinch closed.

Bake at 350°F for 8 to 12 minutes, or until the dough is firm. Let cool for at least 5 minutes, then serve warm or at room temperature.

---

*This recipe can be made with either piecrust, but the Old-Fashioned Gluten-Free Piecrust is easier to work with.

**Savory options include cooked butternut squash and peas, meat and sweet potatoes, or any other vegetable/meat filling you have left over from a previous meal. Sweet options could include chunky fruit purée, peach or apple slices, or pumpkin pie filling (see page 65).

You can make hand pies savory by adding meat, potatoes, onions, parsnips, or peas. Or go sweet with fruit, dark chocolate, or jam.

Pure Cookies, Crumbles, and Cakes

If you are resting and healing your digestive system and body, you know you can't simply gorge indiscriminately on rich desserts. But what if I told you that there were still amazing, delicious, even pleasantly sweet baked goods you *could* enjoy, right here, right now? In this section, I reveal the magical creations that are both mouth-watering and anti-inflammatory.

MY CHOCOLATE CHIP COOKIES! The ones I loved as a child, and missed so desperately after my diagnosis! Well, not exactly, but these cookies replicate those old favorites—and the good news is that they aren't just gluten free, but also completely grain free. Yes, it's true what I am implying here: *You can enjoy chocolate chip cookies, even when you are eating Pure!* They aren't exactly the same, but, if memory serves, I think they might even be a little bit better, especially factoring in how good they will make you feel (and how bad they will *not* make you feel).

The secret is plantains, and just knowing that really makes my day. Plantains are those savory banana-like fruits I use to make pizza crust (page 107), and lo and behold, they can also make killer chocolate chip cookies. When one ingredient can transform into a pizza one moment and a chocolate chip cookie the next and keep you Pure and grain free, I call that magic! This is the secret to chocolate chip cookies that don't cause inflammation. Bake some and share the Pure love.

Makes about 12 cookies

2 large ripe plantains (yellow or black), peeled and chopped

¼ cup solid coconut oil or palm shortening

¼ cup maple sugar or coconut sugar

2 tablespoons cassava flour

1 tablespoon arrowroot starch

1 tablespoon tapioca starch

½ teaspoon baking soda

1 teaspoon ground cinnamon

1 teaspoon ground vanilla bean (or 2 teaspoons gluten-free vanilla extract)

Pinch of ground or freshly grated nutmeg

2 tablespoons raw chocolate chips, unsweetened*

2 tablespoons raw cacao nibs*

Magic Chocolate Chip Cookies

Preheat the oven to 375°F. Line a baking sheet with parchment paper.

Place the plantains in a high-speed blender and blend until smooth. Add the coconut oil, sugar, flour, arrowroot starch, tapioca starch, baking soda, cinnamon, vanilla, and nutmeg. Blend to combine the dough. Stir in the chocolate chips and cacao nibs.

Drop tablespoonfuls of dough onto the lined baking sheet and press down on the tops with the back of the spoon. Bake for 10 to 15 minutes, until the cookies are firm to the touch. Let cool for 10 minutes, then transfer to wire racks or a plate. Enjoy warm or at room temperature. Store the cookies in an airtight container on the counter for up to 24 hours, or in the refrigerator for 3 days.

---

*This recipe calls for raw, unsweetened chocolate chips. These can be hard to find, but I get mine from a company called Pascha (http://paschachocolate .com/our-chocolate/chocolate-chips/sugar-free-chocolate-chips). You could also use raw cacao nibs or break up a raw, naturally sweetened chocolate bar. Just remember to watch the added sweetener while eating Pure.

CACAO NIBS are not chocolate chips. Sorry (I really am!). Chocolate chips contain sugar while cacao nibs do not—but let me tell you, cacao nibs are still a treat. They are raw and manage to stay within the Pure guidelines, which is great news for dessert lovers. Dark, no-sugar-added cacao is actually rich in antioxidants. So, while standard chocolate is a no-no in Pure eating, these flavorful, satisfying macaroons will remind you of all the joy chocolate brings to life.

Makes about 12 cookies

1 cup unsweetened shredded coconut, plus more for sprinkling

1/3 cup coconut flour

1/2 cup full-fat canned coconut milk

1/4 cup real maple syrup

Pinch of ground cinnamon

Pinch of ground vanilla bean (or 1/4 teaspoon gluten-free vanilla extract)

Pinch of Himalayan salt

1/3 cup raw cacao nibs

Coconut–Cacao Nib Macaroons

Preheat the oven to 350°F. Line a baking sheet with parchment paper.

Combine all the ingredients except the cacao nibs in a saucepan and heat gently over medium-low heat, stirring to combine, until warm. Transfer to a bowl and let sit for 2 minutes. Stir in the cacao nibs and mix until everything is combined.

Using your hands, scoop up bits of dough, roll into 1-inch balls, and place on the lined baking sheet. Sprinkle with shredded coconut.

Bake for 12 to 15 minutes, until the tops start to lightly brown. Let cool before removing from the sheet. Store in an airtight container in the refrigerator for up to a week, but I bet they won't last that long.

WHO CAN RESIST warm bubbling fruit with a sweet crunchy topping? Nobody I know. Serve warm or cold with some dairy-free ice cream, or Whipped Coconut Cream (page 126), but I also just eat it the way it is...for breakfast! Get creative, and use any other fruits or berries you like.

Serves 9

Pear-Apple-Ginger Grain-Free Crumble

1 tablespoon palm shortening, nondairy butter (such as Earth Balance), or coconut oil, for greasing the pan

¾ teaspoon Himalayan salt

½ teaspoon ground vanilla bean (or 1 teaspoon gluten-free vanilla extract)

1 tablespoon grated lemon zest

1 tablespoon fresh lemon juice

2 tablespoons real maple syrup

4 pears, peeled, cored, and diced

4 apples, peeled, cored, and diced

½ cup solid cold coconut oil or nondairy butter (such as Earth Balance)

6 tablespoons maple sugar, date sugar, or coconut sugar

½ cup coconut flour

½ cup cassava flour

¼ teaspoon ground ginger

Preheat the oven to 350°F. Grease an 8-inch square baking dish with the palm shortening.

In a large bowl, combine the salt and vanilla. Stir in the lemon zest, lemon juice, and 1 tablespoon of the maple syrup. Add the pears and apples and stir to coat evenly. Spoon the mixture into the baking dish and set aside.

In a large bowl, combine the remaining 1 tablespoon maple syrup, the coconut oil, sugar, coconut flour, cassava flour, and ginger and mix well with your hands until it forms big chunks. Crumble the topping mixture over the fruit in the baking dish. Bake until the fruit is bubbling and the crumble is lightly browned, 45 to 50 minutes. Serve warm or at room temperature. Store covered in the refrigerator for up to 2 days.

ONCE YOU KNOW how to make this whipped cream, I predict you will use it as often as I do. It makes everything taste special, but it keeps you Pure.

Makes about 1 cup

1 can full-fat coconut milk with no emulsifiers or other additives

1 tablespoon real maple syrup, raw honey, maple sugar, coconut sugar, or date sugar

whipped coconut cream

Refrigerate the coconut milk for 24 hours or longer. (You could keep a few cans in the refrigerator at all times so you are always ready to make this.) Meanwhile, chill a metal bowl or the bowl for your stand mixer in the freezer for at least 1 hour before preparing the cream.

Open the entire top of the can and remove it. Using a slotted spoon, scoop out all the hardened cream and put it in the chilled bowl. (Save the remaining liquid for another use, like making smoothies.) Whip on high speed until the cream turns fluffy, slowly drizzling in your choice of sweetener.

Serve immediately or store in an airtight container in the refrigerator for up to 1 week.

ANOTHER CRUMBLE? Yes, please! Crumbles are one of my favorite fruit desserts to make, but the crumble part on top usually contains grain. When I needed a little gut rest, I missed fruity desserts like this—until I created a grain-free crumble.

You can substitute a lot of different kinds of fruit, and the cooking makes the fruit gentle on your digestion. But the apple-berry combination is one of my very favorites. I love how the tart cranberry meets the sweetness of the apple and blueberries, and the way the ground vanilla marries all the flavors together. Also, the apples and cranberries give it an autumnal or seasonal feel, but the blueberries add flavor and beautiful color contrast. If you can't find good blueberries when cranberries are in season, use good-quality frozen organic blueberries. You can use a lot of different kinds of apples; I like to use an assortment of what I can find at the farmers' market or a farmstand, but ask about which varieties are best for baking, rather than eating raw. Some have a better texture and flavor when cooked.

This dessert is infinitely adaptable, so play with it to see what fruits and fruit combinations you like best. Also, while this is more than fine for dessert, I often eat it the next day, cold, for breakfast.

Serves about 8

FILLING

4 medium apples, peeled, cored, and cut into small chunks

1 cup blueberries, fresh or frozen

¼ cup cranberries, fresh or frozen

3 tablespoons real maple syrup

Juice of ½ lemon

1 tablespoon arrowroot starch

½ teaspoon ground ginger

¼ teaspoon ground vanilla bean (or ½ teaspoon gluten-free vanilla extract)

CRUMBLE

½ cup arrowroot starch

⅓ cup coconut flour

2 tablespoons maple sugar, date sugar, or coconut sugar

1 teaspoon ground cinnamon

Pinch of Himalayan salt

½ cup coconut butter or nondairy butter (such as Earth Balance)

Apple-Berry Crumble

Preheat the oven to 375° F.

FOR THE FILLING: In a large bowl, combine all the filling ingredients and stir to combine. Transfer to a 9-inch square baking dish.

FOR THE CRUMBLE: In a large bowl, combine all the crumble ingredients and mix with your hands, squishing larger clumps through your fingers. Keep mixing until you have evenly sized crumbles. Sprinkle the crumble on top of the fruit filling to form an even layer.

Place the baking dish on a baking sheet (to catch any overflow) and bake until the top is browned, 25 to 35 minutes. Enjoy warm from the oven or at room temperature, or cold as a breakfast or snack. The crumble will keep covered in the refrigerator for about 3 days—how will you resist it come breakfast time? I never do!

MY MOM was never one to give us anything like *cake* for breakfast. She believed you needed to start the day healthy, and cake to her was not healthy. Instead, she would make my sister and me the very worst oatmeal imaginable: dry, sticky, and lumpy—yuck. (Sorry, Mom.) My sister would fake being ill just to get out of eating it. Of course, it wasn't quite so traumatic for me, since I loved basically all food, but still, I longed for a Danish, a donut, or even some sugary cereal. I knew there was no chance, but I did dream of the day when I was an adult and could eat whatever I wanted for breakfast.

The joke was on me, since I grew up and found out I was unable to eat any of that stuff...until I learned to make them myself. Now I am finally in a place where, as an adult with celiac disease, I can actually have cake for breakfast! Hooray!

Of course, this cake is nutrient dense: It is packed with fiber and resistant starch from the green banana flour, good fats from the coconut that make it satisfying, and soluble fiber from the apple. The cake is sweetened with just a touch of raw honey and some raisins, so there is no sugar crash to worry about, either. I think it makes a perfect breakfast or anytime snack.

Serves 8

Apple Honey Cake

1 tablespoon palm shortening, nondairy butter (such as Earth Balance), or coconut oil, for greasing the pan

1 cup cassava flour (plus more to sprinkle on the greased pan)

¼ cup coconut flour

¼ cup green banana flour (also called plantain flour)

½ cup arrowroot starch

1 teaspoon aluminum-free baking powder

1 teaspoon baking soda

½ teaspoon xanthan gum

1 teaspoon ground cinnamon

½ teaspoon ground cardamom

Pinch of ground nutmeg

1 teaspoon Himalayan salt

⅓ cup coconut oil

⅓ cup raw honey

¼ cup unsweetened applesauce

1 teaspoon apple cider vinegar

1 teaspoon ground vanilla bean (or 2 teaspoons gluten-free vanilla extract)

¾ cup coconut milk (or nondairy milk of choice)

1½ cups chopped apple

½ cup golden raisins (with no added sugars)

GLAZE

Juice of ½ lemon

1 tablespoon whipped raw honey

Optional: For a thicker glaze, add 1 tablespoon Homemade Powdered Sugar (page 282), but only if your digestion is ready for a bit more sweetener

⟶ recipe continues

Preheat the oven to 350°F. Grease a loaf pan with the shortening and sprinkle with a little cassava flour

In a large bowl, combine the cassava flour, coconut flour, green banana flour, arrowroot starch, baking powder, baking soda, xanthan gum, cinnamon, cardamom, nutmeg, and salt. Use a whisk to break up any lumps.

In another bowl, combine the coconut oil, honey, applesauce, vinegar, and vanilla. Use a stand mixer or hand mixer to beat until combined.

Add the dry ingredients to the wet ingredients a little at a time, alternating with the coconut milk and beating after each addition. Add the apple and beat on high speed for 1 minute. When fully combined, fold in the raisins.

Pour the mixture into the loaf pan and bake for 25 to 35 minutes. The cake is done when a toothpick inserted into the center comes out clean.

While the cake is baking, prepare the glaze: In a small bowl, whisk together the lemon juice and honey.

Place the cake on a cooling rack and let cool. Drizzle with the glaze and serve warm or at room temperature. The cake will keep in an airtight container for about 24 hours, or freeze individual slices for breakfast, snack, or dessert, so you have it whenever you crave it.

℘⟶

RESISTANT STARCH IS YOUR FRIEND

Resistant starch is a kind of starch that doesn't get digested, and this is a good thing. Because it stays undigested in your stomach, it feeds all the good gut bacteria in your colon (this is why it is also called a prebiotic). And because it is not digested, it doesn't make your blood sugar spike and crash, so it helps improve blood sugar and insulin balance.

Green banana flour (also called plantain flour) is one of my favorite sources for resistant starch, so you will see it in several recipes throughout this book.

THIS TREAT is just like its name: pure fruit and chocolate happiness. But I created it out of need. I wanted something sweet, but I was in a hotel room with no kitchen, so I couldn't bake anything. I had bought myself some raw dark chocolate and some coconut flakes for snacking. I don't know if you have ever tried to snack on unsweetened raw chocolate before, but it's just not very pleasant. I wasn't sure why I bought it, until I decided to order some room service: a bowl of mixed fruit and some matches. I proceeded to melt the chocolate with the matches. I actually sat there holding match after match over the chocolate until it was soft. It took forever, but what can I say...I needed chocolate! When the chocolate was soft, I dipped the fruit into the chocolate, dipped it all in some coconut, and put it in the hotel refrigerator (next to the disgusting cans of soda). About a half hour later, I was sitting in the bathtub eating raw dark chocolate–covered fruit. Yes, I was the MacGyver of food! And yes, these are the lengths to which I will go to get myself something both sweet and healthy. When you have the motivation, anything is possible!

The truth is that chocolate is not the enemy. It's all the sugar in it that creates a problem. Actually, raw dark chocolate is very good for you. It's loaded with vitamins B_1, B_2, B_3, B_5, B_9, and E. It is also packed with magnesium and other beneficial antioxidants. On its own, dark chocolate can be bitter, but paired with fruit's natural sweetness, it works perfectly. This treat is pure fruit and chocolate happiness.

Serves 8 to 12

About 4 cups assorted fruit (strawberries, banana, figs, peaches, and/or blueberries)

1 cup dairy-free, raw dark chocolate chips, or 1 approximately 6-ounce bar dairy-free raw dark chocolate, broken in pieces (preferably no refined sugar, no other ingredients)

2 tablespoons real maple syrup

1 tablespoon coconut oil

Pinch of Himalayan salt

1 cup shredded unsweetened coconut

Dark Chocolate Fruit Happiness

Wash the fruit and set it on paper towels to dry completely. Line a baking sheet with parchment paper. In a double broiler, melt the chocolate, adding the maple syrup, coconut oil, and salt. When melted, dip in each piece of fruit, one at a time, then dip in the coconut. Place on the lined baking sheet and refrigerate for at least 30 minutes before eating. These will only keep in the refrigerator for about a day.

HERE IS a fruity version of the squash galette on page 175. It's very rustic, but I adore that: I've never been a stickler for pristine and perfect baking. All you do is press out some dough, put fruit in the center, fold the edges over the filling, and bake. This is a wonderful summertime dessert when you don't want to be in the kitchen baking all day. Try it warm with some dairy-free ice cream or Whipped Coconut Cream (page 126). You could also make it with peaches, nectarines, plums, or apricots.

Serves 6

2 pears, cored and sliced into ¼-inch slices (and peeled, if desired)

1 tablespoon arrowroot starch

2 teaspoons maple sugar, coconut sugar, date sugar, or evaporated cane juice

1 teaspoon ground cinnamon

½ teaspoon ground vanilla bean (or 1 teaspoon gluten-free vanilla extract)

Dough from Grain-Free Piecrust (page 102), chilled and ready to press out

2 tablespoons nondairy butter (such as Earth Balance)

1 tablespoon olive oil

Pear Galette

Preheat the oven to 375°F. Line a baking sheet with parchment paper.

In a large bowl, combine the pears, arrowroot starch, sugar, cinnamon, and vanilla.

Press the chilled pie dough into a 12-inch circle, about ¼ inch thick, on the lined baking sheet. Use your hands, and don't worry about it looking perfect. It should look rustic. Add the filling to the center of the dough, leaving a 2-inch border of bare crust. Dot the filling with little dabs of butter. Fold the edges of the crust over the filling, leaving the filling in the center visible. Brush the crust edges with the olive oil.

Bake for 35 minutes, until the edges are golden brown. Let cool before slicing into wedges and serving. If you have any leftovers, wrap them well and store them in the refrigerator for a day or two.

Clean

RECIPES FOR LIVING

Welcome to Clean eating! Here, you will start including a very small amount of gluten-free grains, nightshade vegetables, and seeds in your diet if you feel like your digestive and immune systems have had sufficient rest. If you've been eating Pure, at this point your bloating and inflammation will have gone down drastically. Your undereye circles will have faded, your swelling subsided, and your energy should be better. Of course, that's *if* you ate Pure for at least a few weeks and observed all the recommendations. Now is a great time to take out that notepad or journal and jot down how you feel each time you add a grain, seed, nightshade, or raw vegetable. This will help you determine what you are ready for, and what you tolerate or may never tolerate.

Clean recipes can become the basis for your go-to, day-to-day meals and snacks. As with all the recipes in this book, and all of the food we serve at Jennifer's Way Bakery and ship around the country, the food in Clean is all gluten free, dairy free, egg free, soy free, corn free, and refined sugar free. It's all safe. There's no guesswork. You'll notice that the recipes are on the lighter side. Healthy fats are great for you, but too much at once can be hard to digest even if you're feeling strong and in the maintenance zone.

You'll see some gluten-free grains, raw vegetables, and beans popping up in this section, and that's fine when you are feeling less inflamed. Just don't overdo it. I would not eat gluten-free grains more than once or twice a day. Listen closely to your body and wait until you feel like your gut lining is recovering before you expand into new food groups. The recipes will be here for you when you're ready.

Clean Smoothies and Plant-Based "Milk" Shakes

You could buy boxes of plant milk in the store, made with fillers and sweeteners. But why do that to yourself when you can make your own pure, clean nondairy milks (sometimes people call them plant milks) at home? Hemp is my favorite seed for making plant milk, and I use Homemade Hemp Milk (page 144) in many of my recipes, including smoothies. And speaking of smoothies, I've got a couple here as well. When you are eating Pure or Clean, smoothies make a great breakfast, snack, or even dinner. These are some of my favorites and I make them often because they are easy to digest and also taste like ice cream.

A SMOOTHIE isn't always the most nutritious choice. Smoothies from the store, or even the ones that juice bars will make for you, are often loaded with sugars and very low in protein. However, if you make your own with hemp milk, all that changes. Start with my hemp milk recipe and add your favorite fruits—mine are peaches and blueberries. I love to buy a bunch of in-season berries and peaches from the local farmers' market and freeze them to use year-round, especially when I'm looking for a burst of sunshine in the middle of winter. This smoothie is not only yummy, but the hemp milk is loaded with protein and fiber and, when mixed with the antioxidants from the blueberries and vitamin C from the peaches, it keeps you smiling all day long. It's also great as a midday, pick-me-up snack.

Fruity Hemp Smoothie

Serves 2

2 cups Homemade Hemp Milk (page 144)

1 cup blueberries

1 whole peach, peeled and pitted (or 1 cup frozen peach slices)

¼ teaspoon real maple syrup

Pinch of Himalayan salt

Pinch of ground vanilla bean (or ¼ teaspoon gluten-free vanilla extract)

Blend all the ingredients for 2 minutes in a high-speed blender. Pour into a glass and drink immediately. You can store extra smoothie in an airtight container in the refrigerator for up to 3 days. Just give it a good shake before you drink it.

THIS SIMPLE SMOOTHIE with the classic combination of strawberries and bananas is quick if you have Homemade Hemp Milk in your refrigerator.

Strawberry Banana Smoothie

Serves 1 or 2

1 frozen peeled banana
2 cups Homemade Hemp Milk (page 144)
1½ cups strawberries
¼ teaspoon real maple syrup
Pinch of ground vanilla bean (or ¼ teaspoon gluten-free vanilla extract)
Pinch of Himalayan salt

Blend everything for 2 minutes in a high-speed blender. Store in an airtight container in the refrigerator for up to 3 days. Shake before enjoying.

IF YOU ABSOLUTELY need chocolate for breakfast or a snack, this is a potent but nutrient-dense way to get there.

Chocolate Hemp Smoothie

1 frozen peeled banana

2 cups Homemade Hemp Milk (page 144)

¼ cup raw cacao powder or nibs (or more if you really like chocolate)

¼ teaspoon real maple syrup

Pinch of Himalayan salt

Pinch of ground vanilla bean (or ¼ teaspoon gluten-free vanilla extract)

Blend everything for 2 minutes in a high-speed blender. Store in an airtight container in the refrigerator for up to 3 days. Shake before enjoying.

MAKE YOUR OWN MILK and stay away from tons of sugars, preservatives, and stabilizers! It is so easy and so nutritious—and it costs much less too. Hemp strengthens the immune system, is loaded with protein; omegas; amino acids; vitamins A, E, and B_{12}; and folic acid, and has other anti-inflammatory properties. I make hemp milk once or twice a week because I use it in so many things—smoothies, baking, and just any time I need milk that isn't coconut milk.

If you can tolerate nuts, you can use the recipe to make almond, hazelnut, pecan, sunflower, or any other kind of nut or seed milk. (If you use larger nuts, chop them up first before measuring.) I personally prefer hemp.

Homemade Hemp Milk

Makes about 4 cups

3 cups filtered water
1 cup hemp seeds
2 fresh dates, pitted
Pinch of Himalayan salt
Pinch of ground vanilla bean (or ¼ teaspoon gluten-free vanilla extract) and/or pinch of ground cinnamon

Combine everything in a high-speed blender and blend until completely smooth. If you want to make it even smoother, line a strainer with cheesecloth and set it over a bowl. Pour the milk through the strainer to strain out all the solids. Honestly, I don't do this. I don't mind tiny bits of goodness in my hemp milk.

Store the hemp milk in a glass jar in the refrigerator, where it will keep for up to 3 days.

CARRAGEENAN

One of the reasons I always make my own plant milk is that almost every boxed plant milk (and many other products) you can buy contains a stabilizer called carrageenan. This is a very common food additive derived from red seaweed. Now, this doesn't sound like a bad thing, and technically it is a "natural" product. However, carrageenan has been linked to digestive problems, and may be a trigger for an immune response such as inflammation. There is even some evidence that it could lead to ulcerations and bleeding. Because it may be particularly bad for anyone who already has digestive or stomach issues, I avoid it completely.

I HAVE the greatest memory of getting the rare and very occasional treat of a chocolate shake when my family went out for dinner. It was even rarer when I was allowed to have one at home, so making them with my dad was an event in and of itself. I would lay out all the supplies and we would spend all afternoon making our masterpieces. They were super-thick and creamy, enough to weigh down even a kid with an endless appetite, like I was.

Now I'm making new milk shake memories, with my updated version of a classic chocolate shake. This is just enough to pour into a very large glass and share, with two straws, soda-shop style.

Old-Fashioned Chocolate Shake

Serves 2

4 dates, pits removed

1 frozen peeled banana

2 cups chilled canned coconut milk (full-fat or light)

2 tablespoons raw cacao powder (or unsweetened organic cocoa powder)

1 teaspoon real maple syrup

Place all the ingredients in a high-speed blender and whip until smooth and thick. Pour into a glass and enjoy life like you used to!

Clean Breakfasts

When you have let your digestion rest sufficiently, you will be ready to start incorporating the recipes from the Clean section into your life. This is the time to get out that notebook and make some notes about how you react as you bring foods back into your diet, like seeds, beans, and a little bit more natural sugar. And even though I call this section "Clean Breakfasts," many of the recipes in Clean can be eaten whenever it suits you. Take this "Breakfasts" category with a grain of sea salt—because while these recipes are traditional breakfast foods, they don't have to be for breakfast, just as recipes in other sections might make good breakfasts for you. This is one of the things I hope to do for you in this book: change the way you think about food. Just because you see the word "pie" or "french toast" doesn't mean it's just for a special occasion or just for dessert or just for breakfast. The ingredients may be fine for you to eat every day or at any time of day. I want you to rediscover and remake food in such a way that nutrition meets function. So forget labels and just look at the ingredients.

WE ARE ON a bacon bender here! This breakfast-friendly twist on standard potato hash uses butternut squash. Studded with crispy bacon, you'll forget all about potatoes. If you can tolerate eggs (unlike me), this would probably be perfect paired with scrambled or fried eggs.

Serves 4

2 cups ½-inch chunks peeled butternut squash

1 teaspoon ground cinnamon

½ teaspoon real maple syrup

1 teaspoon Himalayan salt

1 teaspoon freshly ground black pepper

6 strips organic bacon, preferably pastured

Butternut Squash and Bacon Hash

Preheat the broiler. Line a baking sheet with parchment paper.

Place the squash in a medium bowl and season with the cinnamon, maple syrup, salt, and pepper. Toss to coat.

Scatter the squash evenly over the parchment. Broil for 10 to 15 minutes, until you can easily pass a fork through the squash. Remove from the oven and set aside.

Cut the bacon into 1-inch pieces and cook in a skillet over medium heat, stirring frequently, until just beginning to crisp. Drain any excess oil from the pan (you could save it for future cooking, which I often do). Add the squash to the pan, turn the heat to low, and start mixing everything together with a fork, squashing the squash down and breaking it up until it's all nicely mixed and crispy, 15 to 20 minutes. Serve hot.

HOORAY, it's pancake time! I grew up eating pancakes and I've tried and tried to re-create them without grain. They simply don't come out the same, which is why I don't have any pancake recipes in the Pure section. This was hard for me to digest (so to speak) because I love a good pancake on the weekend. When I was a little girl, not even tall enough to reach the upper cabinets in the kitchen, I would pull a chair over and climb onto the counter and reach up to where my mom kept the pancake mix, and then climb down and make pancakes for the whole family. Of course, those boxed mixes are really nothing more than white flour and sugar, and we will have none of that here. Instead, this recipe, which I created one morning after discovering teff flour, is scrumptious topped with some real maple syrup and honey butter. Teff is an Ethiopian grain that is naturally gluten free, so it is very nutritious. It has a nutty flavor and I think it's beyond delicious. Try these and you'll be starting your day full of fiber, protein, and goodness.

Buckwheat-Teff Pancakes

Makes about 8 pancakes

½ cup buckwheat flour

½ cup teff flour

¼ cup brown rice flour

½ cup potato starch

2 tablespoons aluminum-free baking powder

½ teaspoon Himalayan salt

1 cup rice milk, coconut milk, or any other additive-free, unsweetened nondairy milk

½ cup water

⅓ cup unsweetened applesauce

2 tablespoons grape seed oil

1½ teaspoons real maple syrup, plus more for serving

1 tablespoon palm shortening, nondairy butter (such as Earth Balance), or coconut oil, for the pan

Honey Butter (page 233)

In a small bowl, whisk together all the flours, the potato starch, baking powder, and salt. In a separate bowl, whisk together the rice milk, water, applesauce, oil, and maple syrup. You may need more or less liquid to get the consistency that you like. Add the wet ingredients to the dry a little at a time and mix just until combined. You might need to experiment. A thin crepe-like pancake with fresh strawberry jam in the center is amazing, but a thick hearty pancake topped with warm maple syrup can make me smile just as wide.

Coat a cast-iron skillet with palm shortening and heat over medium heat until it sizzles when you drop a little water into the pan. Pour three or four portions of batter into the skillet a little at a time for smaller pancakes, or make one large pancake. Cook until bubbles start to form in the center of the pancakes, 3 to 5 minutes. Turn and cook until they are cooked through (peek under one with a spatula to check that it is golden brown), 30 seconds to 1 minute. Repeat with the remaining batter, adding more oil to the pan as needed.

Serve warm with Honey Butter and a gooey splash of maple syrup.

WHAT'S INDULGENT if not bacon? Everything's better with bacon. Bacon makes the world go around. People love to make statements about how indulgent and amazing bacon is, and I agree that it is both, but it is also definitely *not* the "devil's food" I once thought it was. In fact, about half the fat in bacon is the monounsaturated kind, which is the same kind that is in olive oil. But even if it's coming from a good clean source—from organic, pastured pigs and cured without nitrates and nitrites—it's still indulgent (it's very high in fat) and I wouldn't eat it every day. But it's actually also a pretty good food, with protein and good fats, in small amounts.

That's exactly how you will find it in this recipe—a small amount of salty, savory bacon sandwiched between two halves of a deliciously sweet and spicy pumpkin biscuit, all slick with maple syrup. This recipe makes fast-food breakfast sandwiches pale in comparison.

And by the way, the biscuits are grain free, so if you decide to skip the bacon, you can enjoy one while you are eating Pure.

Makes 4 to 6 biscuits

½ cup cassava flour

⅓ cup coconut flour

½ cup arrowroot starch

1 teaspoon aluminum-free baking powder

¼ teaspoon xanthan gum

1 teaspoon ground cinnamon

¼ teaspoon turmeric powder

¼ teaspoon Himalayan salt

¾ cup water

¼ cup coconut oil or olive oil

¼ cup organic pumpkin purée

1 teaspoon raw honey

1 teaspoon baking soda

1 tablespoon apple cider vinegar

1 (8-ounce) package organic bacon, preferably pastured

Real maple syrup, for serving

Pumpkin Biscuits with Bacon and Maple Syrup

Preheat the oven to 350°F. Line a baking sheet with parchment paper.

In a large bowl, mix together all the dry ingredients (through the salt). In a separate bowl, combine the water, oil, pumpkin, and honey. Add the wet ingredients to the dry, mixing as you go. In a small bowl, combine the baking soda and vinegar and mix only once or twice (it will be fizzy). Add immediately to the dough and stir in.

With a large spoon, scoop out a big spoonful of dough and plop it onto the lined baking sheet. Wet your hands and smooth the top. Repeat to make 4 or 6 biscuits, depending on how big you want them. Bake until the tops and bottoms are lightly browned, 15 to 25 minutes. Let cool.

Meanwhile, cook the bacon per the package instructions. Drain the bacon of excess grease.

After the biscuits have cooled, carefully break them in half. Divide the bacon between the biscuits and drizzle each with maple syrup before returning the tops and devouring.

BACON-WRAPPED DATES

If you purchased a larger package of bacon and you have extra after making your pumpkin biscuits or your butternut squash and bacon hash, or if you just can't get enough bacon and you want another idea, try this simple but fancy-seeming appetizer, which is always a huge hit at parties. I would never tell you that you can't just make it for yourself, either. This is like bacon candy, seriously.

6 strips organic bacon
12 pitted dates

Preheat the oven to 350°F. Cut each bacon strip in half. Wrap each date in a strip of bacon and secure with a toothpick. Put the bacon-wrapped dates in a baking dish and bake for 15 to 20 minutes, until the bacon is cooked through. You could finish them under the broiler to crisp up the bacon, but watch very carefully because they can burn quickly. They should only need another minute or two.

PEOPLE ALWAYS ask me what I eat for breakfast, or what they should eat for breakfast. It's hard enough when you're gluten and dairy free, but if you don't want to eat grain every day (I certainly don't), it really becomes daunting. This pudding is your answer. Chia seeds are packed with amino acids and protein, and are a great source of fiber and, best of all, they do something wonderful when you add liquid to them. They make a rich and tasty pudding that is a perfect way to start the day. Add the good fat coconut brings to the table and you have a full-package meal. It's easy to make and keeps in the fridge for a few days so you can make it ahead of time and beat the morning rush. It's perfect as an anytime snack as well, or dessert when you need something just a little sweetish after dinner. You can also get creative with this pudding, adding fruit, nuts, seeds, or chocolate, as your digestion permits and your whims dictate.

Serves 4

Coconut– Chia Seed Pudding

2 cups full-fat coconut milk (you could also use light coconut milk, if you prefer a lighter pudding)

1 cup filtered water

3/4 cup unsweetened shredded coconut

1 cup almond milk or hemp milk (at room temperature)

2½ tablespoons real maple syrup (or more if you prefer it sweeter)

1½ teaspoons ground cinnamon

1 teaspoon ground (or freshly grated) nutmeg

½ teaspoon ground vanilla bean (or 1 teaspoon gluten-free vanilla extract)

Pinch of Himalayan salt

½ cup chia seeds

Combine the coconut milk, water, and coconut in a blender. Mix on high speed until creamy. Empty into a small bowl and set aside.

In the same blender, combine the almond milk, maple syrup, cinnamon, nutmeg, vanilla, and salt and blend on high speed until creamy. Pour into a large mixing bowl. Add the chia seeds and whisk briskly. Add the coconut milk mixture and whisk a bit more to combine. Cover the bowl with plastic wrap and refrigerate for 30 to 40 minutes (or overnight) before serving. Store any leftover pudding in an airtight container for up to 3 days.

FRENCH TOAST was a weekend special in our house when I was growing up, so it was out of the question for me that I might never enjoy that gooey, sticky morning treat again. *I would find a way!* But what can you do when you are allergic to the bread *and* the eggs? What's left?

I cracked the code, and this recipe takes me back to my French toast happy place—where I can still enjoy crunchy warm bread fried up to perfection with some yummy maple syrup. The answer was banana and coconut milk, and my Jennifer's Way Classic Artisan Bread. (You can also enjoy this equally with my Amazing Grain-Free Artisan Bread for a Pure feast! Just make the bread without the herbal and salt toppings and it is perfect for this recipe.)

If you have leftovers, freeze individual portions for glorious future breakfasts. Then you can just pop a frozen French toast in the toaster or toaster oven or warm it in a pan in the morning and you're ready to roll. This is high-end fast-food.

Serve warm with maple syrup or any other favorite toppings, like fresh berries, jam, Whipped Coconut Cream (page 126), Honey Butter (page 233), or just have them plain.

Serves 4

4 very ripe bananas, peeled, or 2 cups mixed berries

¾ cup full-fat canned coconut milk

1 teaspoon ground cinnamon

1 teaspoon chia seeds

½ teaspoon ground vanilla bean (or 1 teaspoon gluten-free vanilla extract)

8 large or 16 small slices Jennifer's Way Classic Artisan Bread (page 213) or Amazing Grain-Free Artisan Bread (page 99)

Coconut oil or nondairy butter (such as Earth Balance), for the pan

Banana-Soaked French Toast, Gluten Free or Grain Free

Combine the bananas, milk, cinnamon, chia seeds, and vanilla in a high-speed blender and blend on high speed until fully combined and frothy, about 1 minute. Pour into a flat wide bowl. Put all the pieces of bread into the mixture, and turn each over so they are all completely coated. Let them sit in the mixture for a few minutes, turning them over or switching them around so everything gets well soaked.

Coat a skillet with a few teaspoons of coconut oil and heat over medium-high heat. In batches, transfer the soaked bread slices to the pan and fry them until the bottoms are golden-brown (peek under with a spatula to check), about 3 minutes, depending on the heat of your pan. Flip and cook the second side for about a minute, or until golden-brown. Repeat with all the bread, transferring finished pieces to a warm plate (or to a warm oven).

Clean Salads, Vegetables, and Soup

Now that you've lowered inflammation, you can reintroduce some raw vegetables, nightshades like potatoes, nuts, and gentle legumes like lentils. These foods give you tons of nutrition in every bite, and highlight the gorgeous diversity of veggies you can now enjoy.

POMEGRANATE SEEDS look like little red jewels and give a slightly sweet but tangy contrast to bitter spinach in this colorful salad. Combined with the sweetness of pear, the result is delicious. Those tiny jewels aren't just tasty and pretty, they are also loaded with vitamin C and good for hydrating skin. In fact, you may want to save a few to apply directly to your skin! Compared to green tea, pomegranate seeds are even better for hydration and glow. Go ahead, rub your salad on your face. Consider it one of nature's little gifts.

Spinach, Pomegranate, and Pear Salad

Serves 2

1 ripe pear (Asian pears work great)
1 pomegranate
3½ cups fresh spinach
JW Olive Oil and Lemon Dressing (page 159)
Himalayan salt
Freshly ground black pepper

Cut the pear into slices, and place the slices in a large bowl.

Score the pomegranate with a sharp knife from one end to the other in about 4 lines, like longitude lines on a globe. Then, score around the middle, where the equator would be. Fill a bowl with water and hold the pomegranate under the water. Pull it in half along the equator line, then turn each half inside out under the water, pulling the seeds from the pith with your fingers. Try not to break the seeds, so they retain their juice. The seeds will sink to the bottom and the pith and any old seeds will float. When you've removed all the seeds, pour off the water and pith and drain the seeds. You should have about ½ cup.

Add the seeds and spinach to the pears and drizzle JW Olive Oil and Lemon Dressing over the top. Toss everything together, season with salt and pepper to taste, and serve immediately.

THERE IS NOTHING BETTER than a summer potluck—well, that is unless you look at the spread and realize that everything is off-limits to you. Unless, of course, you BYOS (bring your own salad). As a kid, I couldn't get enough of those creamy, mayonnaise-rich summertime salads. When I host parties or bring my own dish, I always make this Clean crowd-pleaser. The mustard mixes with the oil while the potatoes are still warm, making for a creamy "dressing" that rivals mayo any day.

When using store-bought mustard, remember to double-check the ingredients for hidden gluten. Nobody wants to get glutened at a picnic. I like to serve the salad at room temperature. You can pack it into cute Mason jars and attach a fork with some twine to each and you have a picnic-ready to-go salad.

Serves 4

4 medium or 8 small organic white or yellow potatoes, peeled and cubed

⅓ cup olive oil

1 tablespoon gluten-free mustard

Juice of ½ lemon

2 scallions (white and green parts), chopped

Himalayan salt

Freshly ground black pepper

Picnic-Ready Potato Salad with Mustard Dressing

Place the potatoes in a large saucepan and cover with water. Bring to a boil, reduce the heat, and simmer until a fork can pass through easily but the potatoes are still firm, about 15 minutes. Drain and place in a bowl.

In a small bowl, whisk together the olive oil, mustard, and lemon juice. Pour over the warm potatoes, add the scallions, and mix to coat the potatoes evenly. Season with salt and pepper. Transfer to a serving dish and enjoy! The salad keeps in the refrigerator for 2 days.

VEGETABLE ADORNMENT

Sometimes all I want for lunch or dinner is a fresh green salad or some lightly steamed veggies with a delicious dressing. Great food doesn't have to be hard. The oil in salad dressing actually helps you digest the nutrients from raw veggies more easily, so use either of these tasty dressings the next time you need to add some style to your raw vegetables or salad.

JW Olive Oil and Lemon Dressing

Makes about ¾ cup

½ cup olive oil
Juice of 1 lemon
Himalayan salt
Freshly ground black pepper

Combine all the ingredients in a small bowl or a Mason jar and mix with a whisk or by shaking the *covered* jar. For a little sweetness, you can also add some raw honey.

Ginger-Carrot Sesame Dressing

Makes about 1 cup

3 carrots, cut into large pieces
1 small shallot, peeled
⅓ cup olive oil
¼ cup filtered water
¼ cup apple cider vinegar
2 teaspoons grated fresh ginger
½ teaspoon raw honey
Himalayan salt
Freshly ground black pepper
2 tablespoons sesame seeds

Place everything except the sesame seeds in a high-speed blender and blend until combined. Sprinkle the sesame seeds into a clean Mason jar, then add the dressing on top. Cover tightly and shake. Store in the refrigerator for up to a week.

FENNEL IS one of those vegetables that looks like a mysterious stalk of...*something*. For years, I passed it by in the grocery store because I wasn't sure what it was or what to do with it. Maybe that's you, too. It doesn't look like much, but the slightly licorice taste and health benefits really shouldn't be missed. Fennel is anti-inflammatory, fights bloat, reduces stomach cramping, and is loaded with fiber.

When paired with olives and drizzled with olive oil and lemon, fennel creates an easy dish to put out for guests to enjoy before dinner, serve at a cocktail party, or just enjoy as a snack. It's delicious and clean tasting.

Serves 2

1 whole fennel bulb, tops removed and bulb cut into strips or chunks

1 (4-ounce) can plain black olives (no seasoning), drained

2 tablespoons olive oil

1 teaspoon fresh lemon juice

Kosher salt

Freshly ground black pepper

Fennel and Olive Salad

Place the fennel and olives in a bowl. Add the olive oil and lemon juice, then season with salt and pepper to taste.

Serves 4

THIS SUPER-SIMPLE salad works as a refreshing side dish or as a meal on its own when you add something hearty to the mix: think cannellini beans or even some shredded chicken or tuna. It's also another great bring-along salad for you or your family and friends. I like to take it to the beach because it won't turn sour in the summer heat (of course in that version I wouldn't include chicken or tuna). It travels wells and can be eaten warm, at room temperature, or cold. Enjoy!

4 medium or 8 small organic white potatoes, peeled and cut into bite-size pieces (about 3 cups)

1 handful fresh green beans, trimmed

¼ cup olive oil

Juice of ½ lemon

Small bunch (about ¼ cup) fresh Italian parsley, minced

Kosher salt

Freshly ground black pepper

Potato and Green Bean Salad

Place the potatoes in a large saucepan and cover with water. Bring to a boil, reduce the heat, and simmer for 15 minutes. Add the beans and cook for another 5 minutes or until the beans are tender and a fork can pass through the potatoes but they are still firm. Drain and rinse with cold water. Transfer to a large bowl and refrigerate for 30 minutes.

Add the olive oil, lemon juice, and parsley to the potatoes and beans, and season with salt and pepper. Store leftovers in an airtight container in the refrigerator for up to 3 days.

AS A CHILD, these artichokes were a favorite in my family, but not for me. All I saw was a big green vegetable sitting on my plate, and that was not what my culinary dreams were made of. But the filling, as I called it, was amazing. I would eat all the stuffing and leave the actual artichoke where it stood. Nowadays, I've come around to these prickly veggies and I could literally eat the entire artichoke in one sitting. The tender succulent leaves, the tender heart, the added stuffing—well, you already know how I feel about that part. And as a bonus, they are filled with iron and vitamins.

The artichokes make a fancy side dish, but I've also had one as a complete meal. They don't keep very well, so if you aren't serving 4 people, you can cut the recipe in half—or even quarter it to make just one beautiful artichoke for yourself.

Serves 4

4 artichokes

1 cup Italian Bread Crumbs (page 216)

½ medium yellow onion, finely chopped

1 bunch fresh Italian parsley, stems removed, very finely chopped (about ½ cup)

5 medium mushrooms, stemmed and finely diced

1½ teaspoons Himalayan salt

¼ teaspoon freshly ground black pepper

¾ cup olive oil, plus more for drizzling

1 clove garlic, peeled

Grandma's Stuffed Artichokes

Clean the artichokes by cutting off the pointy tips and bottom stem. Cut so that the artichokes stand upright. Discard any brown leaves.

In a large bowl, combine the bread crumbs, onion, parsley, mushrooms, salt, and pepper. Drizzle in the olive oil, a little bit at a time, stirring as you go to coat the bread crumbs. Carefully pull back the leaves of the artichokes and stuff with the bread crumb mixture, tucking it inside as many leaves as you can.

Place the stuffed artichokes in a large saucepan or stockpot (with a steamer rack or basket if you have one, but it's not strictly necessary). Pour in a cup or two of water (depending on your pot size), enough so that one-fourth of the bottoms of the artichokes are covered. Try not to splash water on your beautiful stuffing job. Place the garlic clove directly in the water. Drizzle the tops of the artichokes with more olive oil and season with salt and pepper.

Cover the saucepan and bring the water to a boil over medium heat. Turn the heat to low, cover, and steam, checking periodically to replenish the water if necessary, for about 30 minutes. To test if the artichokes are done, you should be able to pull a leaf off easily. Serve immediately.

WHEN I WAS A KID, there were certain vegetables that I hated because of the way they smelled when they were cooking. Today, those aromatic vegetables are some of my favorites. One was cauliflower, of whose charms I have already frequently talked about (such as for cauliflower "mashed potatoes" on page 86 and Cauliflower Pizza Crust on page 103). Another was Brussels sprouts. Knowing we were having Brussels sprouts was the opposite of inspiring to me in those days; today I love them. Actually, one benefit of having multiple food allergies or intolerances is that you are forced to experiment with new foods, to find things you can actually eat, and sometimes you rediscover foods you once turned away from and might not otherwise have ever tried again.

These crispy, yummy sprouts are amazing as a Thanksgiving side dish, or just a side, snack, or even a full meal for any day of the week.

Serves 4

1½ pounds Brussels sprouts, stems removed

3 tablespoons coconut oil

1 teaspoon ground cinnamon

3 tablespoons Himalayan salt, plus more to taste

Pinch of freshly ground black pepper

½ cup chopped pecans

¼ cup unsweetened dried cranberries

Roasted Brussels Sprouts with Pecans

Preheat the oven to 400°F. Line a baking sheet with parchment paper.

In a large bowl, combine the Brussels sprouts, coconut oil, cinnamon, salt, and pepper. Spread on the lined baking sheet and roast for 30 minutes. Take the pan out of the oven and carefully add the pecans and cranberries, gently mixing together. Roast, tossing the sprouts once or twice to avoid burning, for another 10 to 15 minutes, until they turn golden and crispy along the edges. Serve immediately.

Leftovers will keep in the refrigerator for about 2 days. When cold, they're a little like a salad.

REMEMBER all those days you spent eating McDonald's fries? Oh boy, I do. It wasn't all that often, but when I did get them, I was in heaven. Those days are long gone, but fries do not have to be a thing of the past. Parsnip fries are a little weird and totally wonderful. They came about when I was craving French fries and wanted a better alternative. I looked in my fridge, saw some parsnips, and this is what came of it: crunchy, lightly sweet, yet nutty fries. They are delicious by themselves, and can be a complete meal because the sunflower butter adds healthy fat and protein.

Serves 4

2 or 3 medium parsnips

3 tablespoons sunflower butter (you could also use almond butter if you tolerate it)

2 teaspoons olive oil

2½ tablespoons sesame seeds

½ teaspoon Himalayan salt

Sesame Parsnip Fries

Preheat the oven to 400°F. Line a baking sheet with parchment paper.

To clean the parsnips, peel the outer layer like a carrot. Cut the parsnips into long thin strips like French fries. In a large bowl, combine the sunflower butter, oil, sesame seeds, and salt. Add the parsnips and mix with a spoon or your hands to coat the strips.

Place on the lined baking sheet and bake until crispy and brown, 35 to 50 minutes, flipping the fries about halfway through cooking.

LENTIL SOUP is an old friend of mine. When I was a struggling actress waiting tables for a living, I would make this perfect soup and it would last me several days. I remember going to a gourmet food market at the end of the day, and experiencing the visual spectacle of premade food and freshly baked bread (back in the days when I didn't realize conventional bread was making my condition worse). At the time, I was living on tips from waitressing so the prices in this store were way beyond what I could afford, but at the end of the day the fresh-baked bread was half off, and I would buy two loaves and a package of lentils (usually with a coupon) and make soup. These days, I mimic that experience with my artisan bread (page 213), which I dip into this luscious soup. It's even better than the "olden days"—and still inexpensive.

You can also top with Parmesan cheese if you are able to eat dairy (I never do, but I know some who can). This is a good, wholesome, honest meal.

Serves 4 to 6

Lentil Vegetable Soup

1 medium yellow onion, chopped
2 carrots, chopped
2 stalks celery, chopped
1 cup green lentils
1 bay leaf (dried or fresh)
5 cups cold water
1 tablespoon olive oil, plus more for serving

2 cups fresh spinach and/or kale (I use fresh, but frozen can be more cost effective and just as nutritious)
3/4 cup chopped mushrooms (I use a mixed assortment)
1 tablespoon Himalayan salt
1/2 teaspoon freshly ground black pepper
2 cups gluten-free pasta or rice (optional)

Note: Lentils are a legume, and that means they could lead to stomach discomfort for some people. Remember your food journal—if this soup gives you trouble, write it down so you can notice whether lentils are a problem in general for you, or if your digestion adjusts.

Combine the onion, carrots, celery, lentils, and bay leaf in a medium stockpot and cover with the water. Simmer over medium heat for about 30 minutes. Add the olive oil, spinach, mushrooms, salt, and pepper. Reduce the heat to medium-low and stir a few times. When the spinach starts to wilt down (about 3 minutes), turn the heat to low and simmer for another 10 minutes. Discard the bay leaf.

Serve hot over gluten-free pasta or hot cooked rice, or just put it in a bowl and spoon it up. I drizzle a little more olive oil on top as well.

Store leftovers in an airtight container in the refrigerator for up to 5 days. It tastes great the next day: Just add some more water if needed, reheat, and eat!

Clean Meals

In pure, we took it easy with meat, but these hearty meals take advantage of comfort foods like chicken and beef as well as gluten-free but grain-containing crusts for a savory galette. The recipes make excellent dinners, filled with nutrition but also with flavor. Or, if you eat your main meal in the middle of the day, you can call it lunch. You can substitute any poultry in the baked chicken recipe and any cubed meat in the stew.

YOU CAN make these sandwiches with bread (I especially like the Golden Raisin–Fennel Bread), or go fancy (and grain free) by stacking the ingredients artfully on a grilled portobello mushroom cap—just throw one on the grill for a few minutes until it has nice grill marks, or brush it with oil and broil it for about 5 minutes.

Makes 2 sandwiches

2 slices bacon, cut in half

4 slices Golden Raisin–Fennel Bread (page 222) or 2 grilled portobello mushroom caps

Fresh tomato slices (optional)

½ avocado, sliced

Bacon Avocado Sandwiches

Preheat the oven to 400°F. Place the bacon on a baking sheet and bake for 15 minutes, until sizzling. Transfer the bacon to a paper towel to absorb excess oil and let cool.

To assemble the sandwiches, place 2 slices of bread or the 2 grilled mushroom caps on a plate. Stack them each with the tomato slices (if using), avocado slices, and bacon. Top with a second piece of bread, or leave open-faced, and consume immediately.

THIS DISH is an old Italian standard that my grandmother used to make when we came to visit her on Sundays for long raucous family dinners. At first, I thought Grandma's baked chicken was only a memory because of the bread crumbs, but I couldn't let a few tiny bread crumbs get between me and old-school chicken perfection! So, I made my own, and you can too. Just use the Italian Bread Crumbs recipe on page 216 and re-create this family-friendly, crowd-pleasing, Sunday-dinner-style, all-in-one dish. My grandmother would be proud.

I like to make the chicken in one of those covered ceramic casserole dishes, but if you don't have one, use a 9 x 13-inch baking pan and cover it with foil. If your chicken pieces are large or you are making a lot, you might want to use a larger roasting pan.

Serves 4

About 1½ to 2 pounds chicken breasts, thighs, legs, or a mix (whatever you like or might be on sale), enough to serve 4

1½ cups Italian Bread Crumbs (page 216)

¼ cup chopped fresh Italian parsley

1 teaspoon dried thyme

2 teaspoons Himalayan salt

1 teaspoon freshly ground black pepper

½ cup olive oil, plus more for drizzling

3 sweet potatoes, peeled and cubed

1 cup peas (preferably fresh, but you could use thawed frozen)

Grandmother's Baked Chicken with Sweet Potatoes and Peas

Preheat the oven to 375°F. Rinse the chicken pieces and pat dry.

In a large ziplock bag, combine the bread crumbs, parsley, thyme, salt, and pepper. Pour in the olive oil and mix to combine. Drop the sweet potatoes into the bag and shake to coat them. Tap the bag on the counter so any excess falls off. Transfer the potatoes to a large baking dish, leaving room for the chicken in the middle.

Working in batches so you don't overcrowd the bag, add the chicken pieces to the crumbs and shake to coat with the remaining mixture. Transfer the chicken to the baking dish with the potatoes and drizzle olive oil on top.

Cover and bake for 30 minutes. Uncover and bake for an additional 20 minutes. Add the peas and cook for another 10 minutes. Cut into one of the chicken pieces to be sure the meat is cooked through. A meat thermometer should register 165°F when inserted into the thickest part. Serve hot. Store leftovers in an airtight container in the refrigerator for up to 3 days.

A GALETTE is like a very informal pie, sometimes made with fruit and sometimes made with vegetables. The sage and butternut squash mixed with the sweetness of the peas is a beautiful combination of flavors—very fall friendly, and perfect for brunch or dinner when served with a salad. The galette can be adapted into mini versions—bake individual portions in smaller tart pans, or use mini tart pans to make appetizers for passing around at a party. These smaller versions should bake in 15 to 20 minutes, until golden-brown.

Serves 6

Savory Butternut Squash and Sage Galette

2 tablespoons ghee, coconut oil, or nondairy butter (such as Earth Balance)

1 onion, thinly sliced

1 cup fresh peas

2 tablespoons chopped fresh sage

2 teaspoons real maple syrup

1 butternut squash, peeled, cut into ¼-inch slices, then cut into thin squares

½ teaspoon ground turmeric

½ teaspoon ground cinnamon

Dough from Old-Fashioned Gluten-Free Piecrust (page 205) (or make the Grain-Free Piecrust, page 102), sweetener omitted, chilled, and ready to press out

1 tablespoon olive oil

Preheat the oven to 375°F. Line a baking sheet with parchment paper.

Coat a large skillet with the ghee (or alternative) and heat over medium heat until it warms and spreads easily around the pan. Add the onion, peas, sage, and maple syrup and stir to coat. Cook, stirring constantly, until the onions are caramelized, about 10 minutes. Add the squash, turmeric, and cinnamon and cook until slightly tender, about 10 minutes. Remove from the skillet and set aside.

Spread out a sheet of parchment and press the chilled pie dough into a 12-inch circle, about ¼ inch thick. Use the flat of your hand and pinch holes back together with your fingers as well as you can. It's supposed to look rustic so don't worry about perfection here. Transfer to the parchment-lined sheet. Add the filling to the center of the dough, leaving a 2-inch border of bare crust. Fold the edges of the crust over the filling, leaving the filling in the center visible. Brush the edges with the olive oil.

Bake the galette for 35 minutes, until the edges are golden-brown. Remove and let sit for about 10 minutes. Serve warm. Store in the refrigerator for up to 1 day.

MY GRANDFATHER and I always had a very close relationship. He was a funny, free-spirited man and a great cook. What a treat it was to arrive home from school to find him in our kitchen making his famous stew. He would start early in the afternoon and then let it cook all day to get extra thick. At dinner, the carrots, the potatoes, and the meat would break up at the slightest touch. I would load up a piece of crunchy Italian bread with sweet butter and sit at that table until every last bite of stew was finished. Times have changed but, in my mind, that stew hasn't. This recipe brings me back to the time with my grandfather, dipping buttered bread into his wonderful stew until I was cleaning out the bowl. Get the leanest organic stew meat you can find and keep the meat down to a few great pieces per serving. Beef, lamb, veal—any rich hearty meat works, and you can save your pennies on cheaper cuts of meat because the long cooking time will tenderize pretty much anything. Make it with bone broth if you have some (I *always* have some and hope you do too—page 73), for even denser nutrition and gut-healing. Load up on the veggies and you can't possibly walk away from this meal anything but full and happy. Serve with either my grain-free or classic artisan bread (pages 99 and 213) and some Honey Butter (page 233) and you've got the real deal.

Serves 6

1½ pounds stew meat (lean, grass fed, and organic if possible), cubed

¼ cup tapioca starch or arrowroot starch

⅓ cup olive oil, plus more for serving

1 small yellow onion, chopped

4 to 5 cups filtered water or Bone Broth (page 73)

5 medium carrots, cubed

3 stalks celery, cut into bite-size chunks

8 medium white potatoes, peeled and cut into cubes

1 bay leaf (dried or fresh)

1 tablespoon Himalayan salt

1 teaspoon freshly ground black pepper

¼ cup tomato paste

1 cup fresh or frozen peas

¼ cup chopped fresh Italian parsley

Pop's Weeknight Stew

Dredge the meat in half the starch and set aside.

Coat a large, heavy soup pot or stockpot with the olive oil and warm over medium heat. Add the onion and sauté until translucent. Add the meat and cook over medium to high heat to brown all over, 5 to 7 minutes. Add enough water to cover the meat completely. Lower the heat and add the carrots, celery, potatoes, bay leaf, salt, and pepper.

Cover with a tight-fitting lid and simmer on low for about 1 hour, stirring occasionally. Add the tomato paste and the remaining starch and stir. Continue to cook, covered, over low heat for at least 2 hours or up to 4 hours. The longer it simmers, the better it is. About 5 minutes before removing from the heat, stir in the peas. Discard the bay leaf.

Top with the parsley and a drizzle of olive oil and serve warm with crusty bread. The stew tastes even better when reheated the next day. It keeps in the refrigerator for about 3 days, or in the freezer for a month or two.

I KNOW this cut of meat can be expensive, especially when organic and grass fed. But in my opinion, it is crucial, if we are going to eat meat, that we know as much as possible about what goes into the meat before it gets to our plates. Local organic farmers are always the best source for meat, if you have them and can find them, but there are some non-local companies producing high-quality organic meat products, too, so ask around and search on your own (I don't want to endorse anyone in particular because quality and service seem to change).

When it comes to beef, the filet mignon is one of the leanest yet most tender cuts you can find, which is great if you like beef but don't want to eat heavier, fattier cuts, which can be very hard to digest.

By the way, I am often asked why I eat meat at all—especially when people see my bakery items, some of which are labeled "vegan" (because they contain no animal products). Yes, I don't want dairy in my bakery because I can't tolerate it, and yes, I *love* animals and I wish I could do without ever eating them. The problem is, I can't eat eggs or dairy, and my body desperately needs protein that is easy to digest.

I eat this meal about once a month, and when I do, I instantly feel more alert and well fed in a way I never quite do with vegetable-based meals. You might be different and you might not feel you need to eat meat, and that's totally fine too. This is about knowing your body and knowing what makes you feel better.

This recipe serves one, but is easy to expand so feel free to multiply the ingredient amounts by however many people you want to serve.

Filet Mignon with Arugula and Fresh Tomato Salad

Serves 1

1 filet mignon (organic, grass-fed beef preferable)

Himalayan salt

Freshly ground black pepper

1 teaspoon plus 1 tablespoon olive oil, plus more for the pan

2 plum tomatoes

2 handfuls fresh arugula or fresh spinach

Thirty to 60 minutes before cooking, take the steak out of the refrigerator, dry it with paper towels, and sprinkle liberally with salt. Let it rest on a plate.

—→ recipe continues

Filet Mignon with Arugula
and Fresh Tomato Salad,
continued

STEAK SECRETS

The secret to cooking a really good steak is for the meat to be as dry as possible. The best way to do this is to take the meat out of the refrigerator 30 to 60 minutes before cooking it (it should already be fully defrosted). Dry it with paper towels as well as you can, then salt both sides of the meat well and let it sit on a plate. The salt will help dry out the surface, so that when you cook it, you will get a nice even surface and a juicy, flavorful interior.

Preheat the oven to 375°F. Brush the steak with the olive oil and season both sides with more salt and the pepper.

Coat an oven-safe (preferably cast-iron) skillet or grill pan with olive oil and heat on high heat. When the pan is hot enough that a drop of water sizzles on its surface, place the steak in the pan and watch the time carefully. Cook for 2 to 3 minutes on each side. You want to let it get a nice crispy exterior. If the steak is very thick, it may need another minute or two. Don't handle the steak too much and only flip once, if possible. Let the pan work its magic.

Remove the pan from the heat and put it directly into the hot oven. (If your pan is not oven-safe, transfer the steak to a baking dish first.) Roast for 5 to 15 minutes, depending on how you like your meat. For rare, 5 minutes is enough; 15 minutes should give you a medium steak. Filet mignon dries out if you overcook it because it has so little fat, so try not to go longer. You can also check the internal temperature with a meat thermometer to confirm your level of doneness—cook it to 140°F in the middle for medium-rare, 155°F for medium. Watch carefully or set a timer so you don't overcook it!

Remove the meat from the oven and let it rest for at least 5 minutes to let the juices redistribute.

While the steak rests, slice or chop the plum tomatoes, place in a small bowl with the arugula, and lightly dress the salad with olive oil and a pinch of salt and pepper. Slice the steak and serve on top of the salad (or alongside it). Enjoy!

I NEVER ATE anything like pork tenderloin growing up. My world consisted of pasta, and then some more pasta, then maybe some chicken, and then more pasta. When I was older, dishes like tenderloin seemed very fancy and out of reach, so I rarely considered making them. However, one night, I was shopping for some inspiration for dinner and came across a pork tenderloin. I decided to go for it. It was so easy to make, I wondered why I never tried it before. It has now become part of my regular repertoire and I often serve it, topped with a tart and fresh chutney, when I have friends over for dinner.

Pork Tenderloin with Cranberry Chutney

Serves 6 to 8

MARINADE

2 tablespoons olive oil

1 teaspoon maple sugar

1 teaspoon chopped fresh thyme

1 teaspoon chopped fresh rosemary

1 teaspoon Himalayan salt

1/2 teaspoon freshly ground black pepper

MEAT

1 pork tenderloin (1 to 1 1/2 pounds)

1 teaspoon olive oil

Cranberry-Maple Chutney or Cranberry-Thyme Chutney (page 182)

Position an oven rack in the middle of the oven and preheat the oven to 450°F. Ten to 20 minutes before you plan to cook your pork loin, place an oven-proof skillet (10-inch or larger, preferably cast iron) in the oven. You want to get the pan and oven nice and hot before you start.

As your pan heats, prepare the marinade: Combine all the ingredients in a small bowl and whisk to combine. Place the pork loin in a dish and pour the marinade over to coat. Let sit at room temperature until ready to cook.

Carefully remove the hot pan from the oven and place it on the stovetop. Drizzle with some olive oil and spread it around the pan to coat. Set the marinated pork in the pan and return it to the oven. Roast for 10 minutes. Flip the pork to the other side, reduce the oven temperature to 400°F, and continue roasting for another 10 to 15 minutes. The pork is done when its internal temperature, in the thickest part of the meat, reaches 140°F to 145°F. Transfer the pork to a cutting board. Tent with foil and let the meat rest for 10 minutes before serving.

When it is ready, carve and serve with the chutney on top. Leftovers will keep in the refrigerator for 3 days.

THIS CRANBERRY CHUTNEY sounds like a holiday dish, but I use it all the time on a lot of different things, from the pork tenderloin on page 180 and baked chicken to crostini. I try to sneak cranberries into my meals whenever possible, as they have so many health benefits, not the least of which is keeping the urinary tract free from harmful bacteria. They are also loaded with antioxidants, fiber, and vitamin C. I buy them when they are in season (fall and winter) and keep them frozen to use in recipes all year long.

Makes about ³/₄ cup

1 cup fresh or frozen cranberries

¼ cup real maple syrup

2 tablespoons filtered water

½ teaspoon fresh lemon juice

Pinch of ground cinnamon

Pinch of ground ginger

Pinch of ground vanilla bean (or ¼ teaspoon gluten-free vanilla extract)

¼ teaspoon Himalayan salt

Cranberry–Maple Chutney

In a small saucepan, combine all the ingredients and bring just to a boil. Simmer for 6 to 9 minutes, stirring occasionally. When the cranberries pop open and soften, the chutney is done. Remove from the heat and let cool, then refrigerate. The natural pectin in the cranberries will help this gel just slightly as it cools. The chutney will keep in a covered glass jar in the refrigerator for up to 3 weeks.

THIS IS a more savory, less sweet, uncooked version of cranberry chutney. It's also good on pork loin and chicken, as well as Thanksgiving turkey. It is quite tangy and wonderful.

Makes about 1¹/₂ cups

½ red onion, diced

1 teaspoon olive oil

1 cup fresh or frozen cranberries, coarsely chopped

2 tablespoons real maple syrup

2 tablespoons freshly squeezed orange juice

1 teaspoon fresh lemon juice

¼ teaspoon ground cinnamon

½ teaspoon chopped fresh thyme

¼ teaspoon ground turmeric

Pinch of Himalayan salt, plus more to taste

Cranberry–Thyme Chutney

Combine all the ingredients in a bowl until fully mixed. Cover and refrigerate for at least 2 hours or up to 5 days.

Clean Pasta, Rice, and Risotto

When I am avoiding grain, I try not to think about pasta or rice too much, but when my digestion is feeling stronger, I love to cook dishes that remind me of my Italian roots—especially interesting versions of spaghetti and risotto. I don't eat them every day, but once a week or so works for me. There are many gluten-free pasta brands available now, but I recommend reading the labels. Many companies want to get in on the gluten-free craze, and although their main pasta line is made from white flour (like semolina), they think they should cash in on the "fad." The problem is, unless they create entirely separate dedicated gluten-free facilities, there is a real risk of cross-contamination. Just because the pasta isn't made of wheat doesn't mean it isn't adulterated with gluten. I prefer smaller companies whose entire operation is gluten-free and who are personally dedicated to quality control. The brands I use are Tinkyada and Andean Dream, but there are other good ones. Try out a few to see which you like the best.

MY OBSESSION with cauliflower continues. This amazing vegetable isn't confined to the Pure section! You can transform cauliflower into so many delicious dishes, but what about just simple cauliflower in its natural form? It is so good, it doesn't even need to look like a pizza (page 103) or mashed potatoes (page 86) to shine. The recipe is quick and easy. You could also eliminate the spaghetti and serve the cauliflower, infused with the turmeric, olive oil, and lemon, by itself or as a side dish to fish or meat. Either way, you've got a powerful, antioxidant-full meal loaded with flavor.

(page 103)

Serves 6 to 8

1 large head cauliflower, leaves and stem removed, chopped into bite-size pieces

2 tablespoons olive oil, plus more for serving

Juice of ½ lemon, plus more for serving

2 tablespoons ground turmeric

Himalayan salt

Freshly ground black pepper

1 pound gluten-free spaghetti

Spaghetti with Turmeric and Roasted Cauliflower

Preheat the oven to 350°F. Line 1 or 2 baking sheets with parchment paper.

Place the cauliflower in a bowl and add the olive oil, lemon juice, turmeric, ½ teaspoon salt, and pepper to taste. Mix until coated.

Scatter the cauliflower evenly on the lined baking sheet. Use 2 sheets if necessary to give the cauliflower space to cook. Roast for 40 to 45 minutes, until a fork can go through it easily.

Meanwhile, fill a medium to large saucepan with water, sprinkle in some salt, and bring to a boil for the pasta. Add the spaghetti and cook according to the package instructions. Drain and return to the saucepan. Add the roasted cauliflower and season with additional lemon juice, olive oil, and salt and pepper to taste. Mix together and serve warm.

CORN-FREE

I avoid gluten-free pastas that include corn, one of the most extensively genetically modified crops out there, as I personally believe that GMO foods are not suited for human consumption.

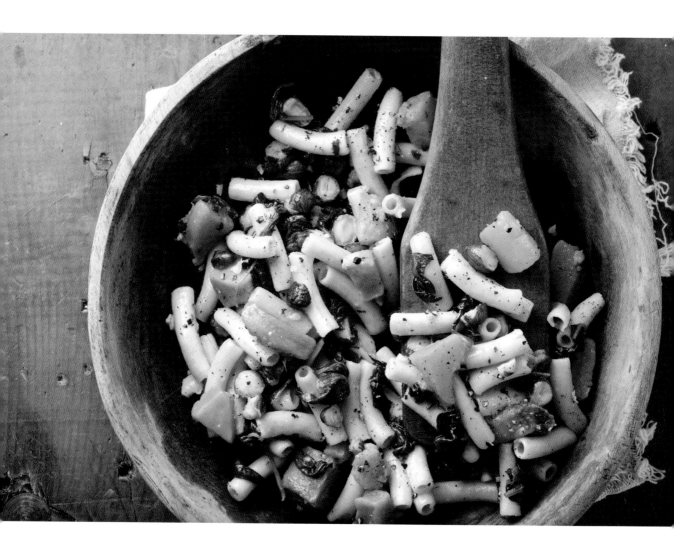

I MADE this pasta one fall evening when I had way too much butternut squash and too little time on my hands. How does anyone pass up those beautiful squashes in the fall? I can't help myself! (At other times when I end up with a squash in every kitchen bowl, I peel and cube them all and store in the fridge in a resealable plastic bag as quick, easy meal add-ins.) In this recipe I pair the squash with sage and some chopped hazelnuts for a complete fall meal. I made this dish for a wedding I helped cater once—all the guests loved it and no one knew it was gluten free.

Serves 6 to 8

1 large butternut squash, peeled and cut into 1-inch cubes

1 tablespoon plus 1/2 teaspoon olive oil

1/2 teaspoon Himalayan salt, or more to taste

1/2 teaspoon freshly ground black pepper, or more to taste

1 cup chopped hazelnuts

2 cups fresh spinach

1 pound any shape gluten-free pasta

Butter-Nutty Pasta

Preheat the oven to 350°F. Line 2 baking sheets with parchment paper.

Scatter the squash cubes on one lined baking sheet, drizzle with 1 tablespoon of the olive oil, and sprinkle with salt and pepper. Roast for about 45 minutes, stirring occasionally, until you can easily pierce a cube with a fork. Scatter the hazelnuts on the second lined sheet and toast in the oven until fragrant, about 10 minutes. Set the squash and nuts aside.

In a small sauté pan, heat the remaining 1/2 teaspoon olive oil over medium-high heat. Add the spinach and cook until it wilts, about 3 minutes, then remove from the heat and set aside.

Meanwhile, fill a medium to large saucepan with water, sprinkle in some salt, and bring to a boil for the pasta. Cook the pasta according to the package instruction until al dente. Drain, return to the saucepan, and toss in the roasted squash, nuts, and spinach. Mix well and serve immediately.

WHEN YOU think of risotto, you probably think of rice, and when you think of rice, you probably assume "gluten free," right? Not necessarily. Depending on what kind of broth or flavoring is used, risotto isn't always safe. Some purchased broths and risotto mixes have hidden ingredients such as thickeners that could include gluten. This is why you must fully read labels or, better yet, make your own so you control the ingredients. As with all risotto, I use bone broth if I have it handy.

This risotto is beautiful for fall, when I am at the peak of my butternut squash obsession. It's an obvious side dish but sometimes I make it my entire meal.

Butternut Squash Risotto

Serves 4

1 whole butternut squash, peeled and cut into small cubes

2 tablespoons olive oil

5 cups Bone Broth (page 73) or chicken or beef broth

1 cup filtered water

1 tablespoon nondairy butter (such as Earth Balance) or coconut oil

1 medium yellow onion, finely chopped

1 clove garlic, minced

1 teaspoon dried sage, or 1 tablespoon finely chopped fresh sage

Himalayan salt

Freshly ground black pepper

1 cup short-grain Italian rice, such as arborio rice

Preheat the oven to 400°F. Line a baking sheet with parchment paper.

Toss together the squash and 1 tablespoon of the olive oil on the baking sheet. Roast, stirring occasionally, until soft and golden-brown, 45 minutes.

In a small saucepan, combine the broth and water and warm over low heat. In a separate large saucepan, heat the nondairy butter and remaining 1 tablespoon olive oil over medium heat. Add the onion and garlic and cook until translucent. Stir in the squash cubes and sage, and season with salt and pepper.

Add the rice, stirring to coat the rice evenly. Turn the heat up to medium-high and slowly start adding a ladle of broth, a little at a time, stirring constantly. The rice should absorb each ladle of broth before you add the next. Keep doing this until the broth is all gone and the rice takes on a thick, soupy consistency.

After adding your last ladle of broth, turn the heat to high and stir for a minute or two so the rice can soak up any extra moisture. This will make your risotto even thicker. Serve hot.

Store leftovers in the refrigerator for up to 3 days. To rewarm, you may need to add a little more broth.

THIS CREAMY risotto uses spring veggies for a fresh crisp flavor—
and no dairy. Yes, you can make risotto without dairy. Risotto
was *not* something I was willing to give up, so I went to work on
a recipe. Many iterations later, I think my creation captures the
magic of risotto without any of the drawbacks. I like to give my
risotto an extra-nutritional gut-healing boost by using bone broth
as the stock. Don't skip the lemon—it really keeps the taste fresh
and light.

Serves 4

Spring Risotto

2 tablespoons nondairy butter (such as Earth Balance) or coconut oil

5 asparagus spears, cut into fourths

5 cups Bone Broth (page 73), or chicken or beef broth

1 cup filtered water

1 tablespoon olive oil

1 medium yellow onion, finely chopped

1 clove garlic, minced

Himalayan salt

Freshly ground black pepper

1 cup short-grained Italian rice, such as arborio rice

Juice of 1 lemon, plus more for serving

½ cup cooked green peas

Grated zest from 1 organic lemon

Heat 1 tablespoon of the nondairy butter in a small sauté pan
over medium-high heat. Add the asparagus and cook for about
5 minutes, until just tender. Set aside.

In a small saucepan, combine the broth and water and warm
over low heat.

In medium saucepan, warm the olive oil and remaining 1 tablespoon
nondairy butter over medium heat. Add the onion and garlic and
cook until translucent. Season with salt and pepper. Add the rice,
stirring to coat the rice evenly. Turn the heat up to medium-high
and slowly start adding a ladle of broth, a little at a time, stirring
constantly. The rice should absorb each ladle of broth before you
add the next. Keep doing this until the broth is all gone and the rice
takes on a thick, soupy consistency. Stir in the lemon juice.

After adding your last ladle of broth, turn the heat to high
and stir for a few moments so the rice can soak up any extra
moisture. This will make your risotto even thicker. Once done,
turn off the heat and fold in the cooked asparagus and peas.
Season with additional lemon juice, salt, and pepper, as needed,
and garnish with lemon zest. Serve hot.

The risotto can be stored in the refrigerator for about 3 days. To
rewarm, you may need to add a little more broth.

ONE DAY, I was in the mood for rice—especially an Indian-inspired rice—but too much grain tends to inflame me and I didn't want to go there. How could I reconcile my two desires? I decided to take some of my favorite anti-inflammatory ingredients and marry them to rice, hoping that would keep the inflammation at bay. And it worked! The result was this amazing dish, which has turned out to be one of my all-time favorites. The combination of coconut and nuts makes this rich enough to be a meal unto itself, but you could also serve it as a side to Baked Wild Salmon in Parchment (page 113). If nuts are a problem for you, simply leave them out.

Serves 4

2 tablespoons chopped walnuts
½ teaspoon coconut oil
¼ teaspoon ground turmeric
¼ teaspoon ground cinnamon
Pinch of cloves
Pinch of freshly ground black pepper
1 cup basmati or jasmine rice, rinsed
¾ cup filtered water
1 cup full-fat canned coconut milk
1 teaspoon Himalayan salt

Coconut Rice

Preheat the oven to 325°F. Line a baking sheet with parchment paper.

Scatter the walnuts on the lined baking sheet and toast in the oven until warm and fragrant, 10 to 15 minutes.

Meanwhile, coat a medium saucepan with the coconut oil and heat over medium heat until it sizzles. Remove from the heat, add the turmeric, cinnamon, cloves, and pepper, and let sit for 2 minutes.

Add the rice to the pan and stir to coat evenly. Add the water and coconut milk, place over high heat, and bring just to a boil. Cover and reduce the heat to low. Simmer for 15 to 20 minutes, until the rice is tender. Fluff with a fork, fold in the walnuts, and season with salt. Serve warm. The rice will keep covered in the refrigerator for about a week.

Clean Cookies, Crumbles, Pies, and Cakes

Now for my favorite part—baking with gluten-free flours. While I am grateful and amazed at what good results I can get from grain-free baking, I also really enjoy baking with gluten-free grains. This is its own kind of challenge, and I have been working on perfecting the art for years now. This is a collection of some of my favorite everyday treats, from pancakes to cupcakes. Have fun with this part, just don't overdo it. You can sweeten your life with the treats, but too much grain can be a burden, so keep it light and make it special.

I NEVER LIKED the taste of pumpkin until I was an adult. Nowadays, I make everything with it! A vital binder for those who love to bake but are allergic to eggs, pumpkin is packed with fiber and vitamin A. And the hazelnut flour in the cookie adds healthy anti-inflammatory oils and a beautiful flavor. These cookies are one of the top sellers at my bakery. We top them with cinnamon sugar or even dip them in chocolate.

Makes about 2 dozen cookies

Pumpkin Spice Cookies

1 cup cassava flour

¼ cup coconut flour

¼ cup hazelnut flour

½ cup arrowroot starch

½ cup coconut sugar, date sugar, or maple sugar

1 teaspoon aluminum-free baking powder

1 teaspoon baking soda

1 teaspoon xanthan gum

1 teaspoon ground cinnamon

½ teaspoon ground cardamom

½ teaspoon ground vanilla bean (or 1 teaspoon gluten-free vanilla extract)

¼ teaspoon freshly grated nutmeg

Pinch of ground cloves

½ teaspoon Himalayan salt

¾ cup organic pumpkin purée

⅓ cup real maple syrup

6 tablespoons palm shortening

3 tablespoons unsweetened applesauce

In a medium bowl, combine all the dry ingredients (through salt) and whisk to get out all lumps. In a separate large bowl, combine the remaining ingredients and mix in a stand mixer or with a hand mixer.

Pour the dry ingredients into the wet a little at a time, combining as you go. Refrigerate for about 30 minutes or longer.

Preheat the oven to 350°F. Line 2 baking sheets with parchment paper (or bake in 2 batches).

Scoop up a teaspoon at a time of the batter and place on the lined baking sheet. Bake for about 20 minutes, until the cookies are firm to the touch but not too hard. Remove from the oven and allow to cool.

THIS COOKIE is named after a little girl I met in my bakery who had become extremely ill due to undiagnosed celiac disease. Lauren had multiple food allergies and her dad wanted her to be able to enjoy a treat on her days off from hospital treatment. So, I took to the kitchen and worked on a very simple cookie that was still nothing short of spectacular for my new little friend. Her dad wrote me to tell me how excited Lauren was to have a cookie all her own—one that she could actually eat! The next time they came in, we chatted, Lauren and I, about how living with autoimmune problems and food allergies is hard, but by the time she left the bakery with those cookies, everyone was smiling. Everyone deserves to smile, and have a cookie, so I hope you will try this one and let it make you smile too.

The Lauren Cookie

Makes about 2 dozen cookies

1 cup hazelnut flour

1 cup quinoa flour

¼ cup arrowroot starch

¾ cup certified gluten-free oatmeal

½ cup maple sugar, coconut sugar, date sugar, or evaporated cane juice

½ teaspoon aluminum-free baking powder

¾ teaspoon baking soda

½ teaspoon ground cinnamon

1 teaspoon Himalayan salt

2 very ripe bananas, peeled

¼ cup grape seed oil or canola oil

½ cup almond milk

½ cup chopped walnuts or pecans (optional)

Preheat the oven to 375°F. Line 2 baking sheets with parchment paper (or bake the cookies in 2 batches)

Combine all the dry ingredients (through salt) in a large mixing bowl. Sift out any lumps with a whisk.

In a separate bowl, mash the bananas with a fork, then add the oil and milk and mix until creamy. Add the wet ingredients to the dry and stir until combined. Fold in the nuts (if using).

With a spoon, scoop out approximately 2-tablespoon portions of the dough and place on the lined baking sheets. Bake for 13 to 16 minutes, or until they are firm—depending on how soft you like your cookies. Note that any time you are baking or cooking with nuts, you can expect your items to get more brown in color. Enjoy!

I THINK everyone has a fond memory of their first oatmeal cookie. Whether home-baked or store-bought, the classic oatmeal raisin cookie is about as old-school-goodness as you can get. The cinnamon mixed with oats and sweet raisins make these cookies just melt in your mouth. While oats are naturally gluten free, sadly they are almost always contaminated with gluten as they are often grown among, or processed with, gluten-containing grains. That's why it is absolutely essential to make these cookies using only certified gluten-free oats—check your oat label (and then check again). When you know you are good to go, start baking these little gems.

Makes 12 cookies

Oatmeal Raisin Cookies

2½ cups certified gluten-free oats

1 cup brown rice flour

¼ cup sorghum flour

½ cup arrowroot starch

½ teaspoon aluminum-free baking powder

½ teaspoon baking soda

½ teaspoon xanthan gum

½ cup maple sugar, coconut sugar, date sugar, or evaporated cane juice

1 teaspoon ground cinnamon

½ teaspoon Himalayan salt

½ cup unsweetened applesauce

½ cup real maple syrup

½ cup olive oil or grape seed oil

½ cup raisins

½ teaspoon ground vanilla bean (or 1 teaspoon gluten-free vanilla extract)

Combine all the dry ingredients (through salt) in a medium bowl.

Using a stand mixer with the whisk attachment, combine the applesauce, maple syrup, olive oil, raisins, and vanilla. Slowly add the dry ingredients to the wet ingredients and mix at low speed until thoroughly incorporated. Chill the dough for at least half an hour.

Preheat the oven to 350°F. Line a baking sheet with parchment paper.

Scoop the dough with a spoon and drop onto the baking sheet. Repeat to make 12 cookies. Press down on the dough tops slightly to flatten. Bake for about 10 minutes, just until beginning to turn golden. If you like a crunchy cookie, wait for them to turn darker golden-brown, about 15 minutes. These cookies will keep for about 3 days wrapped in the refrigerator.

THIS IS ANOTHER cookie that sells out in a flash every time we make a batch at the bakery. I think it's the flavor of the hazelnuts mixed with the chocolate and banana. Hazelnuts have always been a favorite nut of mine, and they are actually very good for your digestive health. They aid in muscle, skin, and bone health too. I like to use raw dark chocolate chips, or even break up pieces of a raw chocolate bar. Raw chocolate isn't always the best on its own when it has no sugar, but put it into cookie dough and it takes on a whole new dimension. Give these a try—they melt in your mouth.

Makes about 12 small cookies

¼ cup hazelnut flour

¼ cup arrowroot starch

¼ teaspoon baking soda

¼ teaspoon ground cinnamon

¼ cup dairy-free, naturally sweetened (or unsweetened) dark chocolate chips or chopped raw chocolate bar

1 very ripe banana, peeled and mashed

2 tablespoons sunflower seed butter (or almond or peanut butter, if you tolerate it)

1 teaspoon real maple syrup or raw honey

¼ teaspoon ground vanilla bean (or ½ teaspoon gluten-free vanilla extract)

Pinch of Himalayan salt

Chocolate Chip–Banana–Hazelnut Cookies

Preheat the oven to 350°F. Line a baking sheet with parchment paper.

Combine all the ingredients in a large bowl and mash together with a fork.

Scoop portions of the dough with a teaspoon onto the lined baking sheet and flatten with the back of a spoon. Bake for 15 to 20 minutes, until browned, but not too hard. Let sit for 10 minutes before enjoying.

These cookies will keep wrapped in the refrigerator for about 3 days.

I TEND TO go a little overboard on fruit in the summer months. I used to rent a home out by the beach in the summer, a few hours from my place in New York. One of my favorite things about the drive out there was stopping at the organic farmstands along the way. The fruits and veggies were overflowing on the tables and I was like a kid in a candy store. In fact, when I was a kid, my grandfather always said that my eyes were bigger than my stomach, and grown-up me at the farmstands proves his point.

At that sweet spot when both wild blueberries and peaches are in season, I am literally singing. I bake the blueberries into pies, grill the peaches and freeze them for smoothies—and put the two together in this amazing crumble. Serve warm with your favorite nondairy ice cream, at room temperature with Whipped Coconut Cream (page 126), or cold after a late night at work. Or have it for breakfast—I do!

Serves about 8

Farmstand Fruit Crumble

Note: Grate your lemon zest before juicing your lemon. It will be much easier.

FILLING

3 firm, ripe peaches

¼ cup Jennifer's Way Bakery All-Purpose Flour Mix (purchased or page 211)

1 teaspoon grated lemon zest

2 tablespoons fresh lemon juice

2 tablespoons real maple syrup

2 tablespoons maple sugar, date sugar, or evaporated cane juice

¼ teaspoon ground vanilla bean (or ½ teaspoon gluten-free vanilla extract)

Pinch of Himalayan salt

1 cup fresh blueberries

CRUMBLE

1 cup Jennifer's Way Bakery All-Purpose Flour (purchased or page 211)

½ cup cold nondairy butter (such as Earth Balance) or coconut oil

¼ cup maple sugar, coconut sugar, date sugar, or evaporated cane juice

2 tablespoons real maple syrup

¼ teaspoon ground cinnamon

Preheat the oven to 350°F.

FOR THE FILLING: Clean the peaches, remove their pits, and cut into wedges. In a large bowl, mix together the peaches, flour, lemon zest and juice, maple syrup, maple sugar, vanilla, and salt. Gently fold in the blueberries. Spoon the filling into an 8- or 9-inch square baking dish (or individual-size ovenproof ramekins).

→ recipe continues

Farmstand Fruit Crumble,
continued

FOR THE CRUMBLE: In a large bowl, combine all the ingredients and mix with your hands, squishing larger clumps through your fingers. Keep mixing until you have evenly sized crumbles. Sprinkle the crumble on top of the fruit mixture to form an even layer.

Place the baking dish (or ramekins) on a baking sheet (to catch any overflow) and bake for 40 to 45 minutes (or about 30 minutes for ramekins). When the fruit is bubbling gently and the topping is golden-brown, the crumble is done.

The crumble will keep, covered in the refrigerator, for about 3 days (remember what I said about having this for breakfast)!

I ASSOCIATE EVERY HOLIDAY and every new season with some kind of pie: fresh wild blueberry in the summer, pumpkin in the fall, rhubarb in the winter, and in the spring, well, pick any fruit! This particular piecrust is stronger than the more delicate Grain-Free Piecrust in the Pure category, so it can handle heavier, denser fillings.

Old-Fashioned Gluten-Free Piecrust

This recipe includes both the piecrust flour, which you can make in bulk and have at-the-ready, as well as a basic piecrust recipe that uses this flour.

↪ piecrust flour

Makes 3 cups (double the recipe for a double piecrust or to make in bulk to store)

1¼ cups brown rice flour
¾ cup sorghum flour
½ cup arrowroot starch

¼ cup tapioca starch
¼ cup quinoa flour

Mix everything together in a bowl, whisking until well blended. Store in an airtight container in the fridge for up to a month.

↪ piecrust

Makes 1 piecrust

3 cups piecrust flour
¼ cup maple sugar, date sugar, coconut sugar, or evaporated cane juice (omit for savory recipes)
6 tablespoons millet flour

1½ teaspoons xanthan gum
¾ teaspoon Himalayan salt
1¼ cups cold Earth Balance nondairy butter
¾ cup cold rice milk

Preheat the oven to 350°F. In a stand mixer with the paddle attachment, combine the piecrust flour, sugar, millet, xanthan gum, and salt and mix on low speed to smooth out any lumps. Add the Earth Balance in small chunks and continue to mix. When the dough starts to look like a crumble, add the rice milk. Turn the mixer to medium speed and mix until the dough starts to stick together. Scoop the dough into a ball and wrap in plastic wrap. Refrigerate for 20 minutes before using in any recipe calling for piecrust.

To prebake this crust, preheat the oven to 350°F. Roll out or just press the dough into the pie plate. Bake the crust for about 12 minutes or until firm and just beginning to turn a very light golden color.

I HAVE A CARROT CAKE I make for special occasions in the Indulgent section of this book (see page 289), but I can't possibly bear the thought of going without carrot cake at any time in my life, so I had to create a grain-free version for my times of digestive rest and healing. That's why I call this my *everyday* carrot cake. Although many grain-free cakes use tons of nuts (such as with almond "flour"), I don't digest those well, and I know I'm not the only one, especially in such quantities. This cake is, therefore, both grain free and nut free, but still contains that wonderful, carrot-y, spicy goodness.

I made the cake for a small group of friends recently, and it was literally gone in minutes. Yes, the entire cake! Two out of the five people had food allergies or celiac disease, and everybody remarked on the light, airy quality and the classic carrot cake flavor.

Serves 8

Everyday (Grain-Free) Carrot Cake

1 tablespoon palm shortening, nondairy butter (such as Earth Balance), or coconut oil, for greasing the pan

1 cup cassava flour, plus a little more for the pan

1/4 cup coconut flour

1/4 cup hazelnut flour

1/2 cup arrowroot starch

3/4 cup maple sugar or coconut sugar

1 1/2 tablespoons aluminum-free baking powder

2 teaspoons baking soda

1 teaspoon xanthan gum

2 teaspoons ground cinnamon

1/2 teaspoon ground or freshly grated nutmeg

Pinch of ground cloves

1 teaspoon Himalayan salt

1 cup mashed ripe banana (about 2 medium bananas)

1 cup coconut oil

1/3 cup unsweetened applesauce

1/3 cup real maple syrup

1 teaspoon apple cider vinegar

1/2 teaspoon ground vanilla bean (or 1 teaspoon gluten-free vanilla extract)

2 cups shredded carrot

HONEY ICING

3/4 cup palm shortening, coconut oil, or nondairy butter (like Earth Balance)

1/4 cup coconut butter

2 tablespoons raw honey

1 tablespoon fresh lemon juice

Pinch of ground vanilla bean (or 1/4 teaspoon gluten-free vanilla extract)

Preheat the oven to 350°F. Grease a Bundt pan or a 6- to 8-inch round pan with the shortening and sprinkle with cassava flour.

In a large bowl, combine the cassava flour with all the remaining dry ingredients (through salt).

In the bowl of a stand mixer with a whisk attachment, combine the banana, coconut oil, applesauce, maple syrup, vinegar, and vanilla and mix until smooth. Slowly add the dry mixture to the wet, whisking at medium speed until combined. Fold in the shredded carrot.

Pour the batter into the pan and bake for 25 to 35 minutes, until a toothpick inserted into the center of the cake comes out clean. Let cool on a cooling rack.

FOR THE HONEY ICING: Whip all the ingredients together until smooth and fluffy.

Top the cake with the honey icing and serve. This cake will keep covered in the refrigerator for up to 2 days.

Indulgent

RECIPES FOR SPLURGING
(IN MODERATION)

What do you think of when you hear the word "indulgent"? Do you think of things that are bad for you? Eating too much? Eating sweet and starchy foods like cakes, cookies, pies, and bread? What if I told you that indulgent doesn't have to be bad for you?

After years baking and working and serving little slices of heaven in my bakery, I still see people eyeing their third cookie and muttering things like, "Oh no, I can't, it's too fattening." I always answer with something like, "If I broke down everything that is in that cookie for you, you wouldn't even think about saying no, because you would be saying no to quinoa, brown rice, chia seeds, applesauce..." We are conditioned to think that if something looks and tastes good, then it must be bad for us, and if something looks and tastes bad, only then can it be good for us. But I'm here to tell you and show you that this just isn't the case.

It has become my mission to continue to enjoy "indulgences," yet still maintain my health, obey the demands of my allergies and autoimmunity, and get nutritional benefits out of *everything* I eat. Even cookies. Even cupcakes. Even French toast.

Now, this is not to say that you should eat at my bakery every day for breakfast, lunch, and dinner. Indulgences are meant to be enjoyed in moderation— too much sweetener, even the natural kind, as well as too much rich meat and too much grain, can aggravate inflammation in some people, especially those with autoimmune issues. That's why I want you to indulge, but I want you to do it rationally and not so much that it makes you feel worse. For me, that means I usually only enjoy these recipes a couple of times a month. For you, that might mean more or less often. This is all about learning what your body wants, and when. But no matter how often you indulge, these recipes are sure to thrill you. They will also amaze the people you cook for, and help you remember how to enjoy the little things in life without compromising your health. Many of them originated in my bakery, and have made people very happy. Now it's your turn.

Indulgent Breads and Baking Mixes

I placed the grain-heavy recipes in Indulgent because, for some people, they may still cause some inflammation. In order to keep inflammation at bay, you may need to use all grains sparingly. If you find that these healthy grains don't cause inflammation for you, then eat to your heart's content. I have found that for me, eating a whole loaf of my bread isn't the best, even though I *love* it. I have to be more conservative when eating bread, so I only allow myself one or two pieces. Again, remember to keep your notebook on hand to record how your body feels with any dietary changes you make.

MANY OF THE RECIPES in the Clean and Indulgent sections use my Jennifer's Way Bakery All-Purpose Flour. It's a convenient product that flies off the shelves at the bakery, and I use it often at home.

There are many gluten-free all-purpose flour mixes out there. Some are just a combination of starches mixed together. Others contain loads of nuts. I personally can't overdo it on either starch or nuts, and I don't want to either. The starch mixtures have absolutely no nutritional value whatsoever and are often loaded with sugar. The nut mixtures are usually mostly almond flour and require using many eggs, and I can't do that either. Nobody should be eating nuts in that volume, and many of us could never digest that comfortably.

So, I created this flour mix out of pure need. My body was so nutrient deficient from my many of years of having celiac disease before my diagnosis that I needed nutrition in everything I ate, and that included bread and dessert, so I set out to make the most nutrient-packed flour possible that still performed the way I needed it to perform. I wanted to use it to create muffins and cookies and cakes and more.

It took many trials and failures, but I finally figured out the precise mixture that would work in all my baking recipes. Once you start baking with the flour, you will see how much easier it makes baking, not to mention life. Some of these specialty flours are a little pricey, but you will definitely use them up as you continue to remake this mix, so it's worth the investment for your convenience and your health. This flour mix is much more nutrient dense than the gluten-free baking mixes you find in stores, and the baked goods you make from it will taste delicious. (Use it for everything except bread—the Bread Flour Mix on page 212 is perfect for that purpose.)

Notice that in this book I often specifically call for Jennifer's Way Bakery All-Purpose Flour Mix. That is the mix you can buy from my website, but now you can also make it in your very own kitchen. For that matter, you can also use either the homemade or purchased mix in place of any gluten-free flour mix in recipes in other books. I predict you will make and use this often.

Jennifer's Way Bakery All-Purpose Flour Mix

Makes 4 cups

1 cup sorghum flour
1 cup quinoa flour
½ cup amaranth flour
¾ cup arrowroot starch
¼ cup potato starch
1½ teaspoons xanthan gum

In a large bowl, combine all the ingredients with a whisk. Store in an airtight container in the refrigerator for up to 1 month.

MY Jennifer's Way Bakery All-Purpose Flour Mix is perfect for making muffins, cookies, cakes, and other sweet treats, but this mix is superior for the sole purpose of making delicious, tender, gluten-free *bread*. Although none of the recipes in this book actually call for this mix, I include it here so you can use it as a substitute for *any bread recipe* that you used to make and love before you gave up gluten. If you normally made it with gluten, try it with my bread flour and you may be quite pleased with the result. You can also use it in any recipe that calls for a commercial gluten-free bread mix. Consider it your secret weapon for converting recipes into gluten-free versions.

I used the bread flour mix as a starting point for getting creative and inventing my own versions of bread. I've used it to make cinnamon raisin bread, chocolate bread, and focaccia, just to name a few. I suggest making a large batch and keeping it in a container in the refrigerator for easy experimenting.

Makes 6 cups

2 cups cassava flour
1½ cups garbanzo bean flour
1 cup millet flour
1 cup potato starch
½ cup sorghum flour

Bread Flour Mix

Whisk all the ingredients together. Store in an airtight container in the refrigerator for up to 1 month. Use cup for cup as a replacement for regular bread flour in any recipes for bread.

THIS RECIPE was *the reason* I started my whole journey into cooking and baking. I wanted to eat a good piece of bread! That's all I wanted. Sounds simple, right? Oh, so very, very wrong. We all know that in a gluten-free world, *good* and *bread* don't usually go together. But I considered it my personal mission to change all that.

This is the result, and the bread goes above and beyond. Not to brag, but I'm seriously so proud to say that Mario Batali, the wonderful celebrity chef, has tasted this bread and thought it was incredible. It has the crunch, the texture, the mouthfeel, and the chew that you remember from your pre-diagnosis life. I could literally eat an entire loaf in one sitting. Who am I kidding, I actually have! (Although I don't recommend this if you need to go easy on all grains—I only do this when I feel like I can handle it.)

If there is one recipe you make in this book, I hope it's this one. You can also give your bread an extra crunch by baking it on a pizza stone. And go ahead with your creativity—this bread can be made into big loaves, small loaves, dinner rolls, baguettes, or any shape you like. Add a cup or two of nuts and raisins (like in the Raisin Pecan Bread recipe on page 219) or anything else you like— snipped apricots, orange peel, dried cranberries, other nuts or seeds, or two tablespoons of raw cacao powder or nibs. It is the palette and you are the artist. Just remember to adjust the cooking time for size. The smaller the bread, the quicker it will bake.

Makes four 6-inch round loaves

2 cups warm filtered water

1/3 cup olive oil

3 tablespoons raw honey or real maple syrup

2 teaspoons apple cider vinegar

2 tablespoons active dry yeast

1/3 cup chia seeds

1 1/2 cups room-temperature water

2 cups millet flour

1 1/2 cups sorghum flour

1/2 cup brown rice flour

1 1/2 cups tapioca starch

1 1/2 cups potato starch

1 1/2 tablespoons xanthan gum

1 tablespoon Himalayan salt

Optional toppings: sesame seeds, chia seeds, rosemary, Himalayan or kosher salt

Jennifer's Way Classic Artisan Bread

Preheat the oven to 390°F. Line a baking sheet with parchment paper.

In a small bowl, mix together the warm water, olive oil, honey, and vinegar. Stir in the yeast and set aside for at least 5 minutes. It should start to look a little bit foamy; this means the yeast is activating.

In a separate small bowl, mix the chia seeds with the room-temperature water. Set aside for a few minutes.

In a stand mixer with a paddle attachment, mix the flours, starches, xanthan gum, and salt until just combined. Add the yeast mixture and then the chia seed mixture. Mix on medium speed for 2 to 3 minutes, until the ingredients are fully combined and hold together just enough that you can scoop the dough out with your hands.

→ recipe continues

Using your hands, shape the dough into 4 round shapes on the lined baking sheet. (You can also do 1 big round or shape the dough into baguettes, or any shape you like, such as dinner rolls.)

Using a knife, score the top of the bread (an X for round loaves, diagonal slashes for long shapes) and sprinkle with your topping of choice, or leave as is without toppings.

Bake the loaves for 40 minutes, then check the internal temperature with a meat thermometer. When it reaches 200°F, the bread is done. If it's not up to temperature, keep baking until you've reached 200°F; it is the best sign of doneness. (Smaller rounds, like dinner rolls, and elongated loaves, like baguettes will likely need less time to reach 200°F. Start checking at 20 minutes.)

Cool completely before slicing. Store any leftover bread on the countertop in a brown paper bag for up to 4 days, or wrap tightly in foil and freeze for up to 1 month. When you take it out of the freezer, reheat it in the oven at 325°F.

THIS IS one of those staple pantry items you totally took for granted before going off wheat and gluten. I bet you didn't even realize that those little crispy crunchy specks give flavor and texture to some of your favorite dishes. I didn't. But I was determined to have all those foods again, like Grandmother's Baked Chicken with Sweet Potatoes and Peas (page 172) and Grandma's Stuffed Artichokes (page 162). The bread crumbs are simple to make—you can start by baking one of my grain-free or gluten-free breads (pages 99, 213), or take a shortcut and purchase some (high-quality) bakery-made gluten-free bread. Either version will help you re-create those old favorites come dinnertime.

Makes 2 cups

1 large loaf homemade or purchased gluten-free or grain-free artisan bread (preferably day-old bread)
1 teaspoon dried rosemary
1 teaspoon Himalayan salt
½ teaspoon garlic powder

Italian Bread Crumbs

Preheat the oven to 375°F. Line a baking sheet with parchment paper.

Using a serrated knife, cut the bread into ¼-inch cubes. Place the cubes in a food processor or blender and pulse for about 1 minute to create a coarse crumb. Add the seasonings and pulse to combine.

Spread the crumbs evenly on the lined baking sheet. Bake until golden-brown, 10 to 12 minutes, tossing the crumbs halfway through baking.

If you don't use them all at once, store in an airtight container in the refrigerator for up to 10 days.

MAKE THESE crunchy gems with leftover bread, if you ever have any. They work with grain-free or gluten-free bread—in fact, with any bread recipe in this book. You can use them in lots of different ways—pop them into salads, sprinkle them on top of soups, crush them down to coat chicken or fish, or use them for good old-fashioned bread stuffing in your Thanksgiving turkey.

You can make as much or as little as you want. It's quick, so you can make croutons a little at a time as you need them, or make a big batch and keep them in an airtight bag in the freezer. You can also experiment with seasonings. Make these your own.

Gluten-Free Croutons

Yield depends on how much bread you use

Any of the artisan bread recipes in this book (pages 99 and 213), or any grain-free or gluten-free bread, in any amount

Enough olive oil to brush over all the bread

Your favorite herbs

Himalayan salt

Freshly ground black pepper

Preheat the oven to 350°F. Line a baking sheet with parchment paper.

Slice the bread into ½-inch slices or cut into cubes and place on the lined baking sheet. Brush with olive oil and sprinkle with seasonings. Bake until lightly browned, about 20 minutes. Flip and brown the other sides, about 20 minutes.

THIS BREAD brings up a lot of memories for me. When I was fresh out of high school, I briefly attended college before realizing that acting school was where I needed to be full-time. I moved into Manhattan, enrolled in acting school, and started waiting tables on the graveyard shift—11 p.m. to 5 a.m.—to put myself through acting school, because money was tight. I had a dear friend whose family owned a French restaurant up the street from my very "cozy" 400-square-foot, fifth-floor walk-up. Whenever I had the chance, I would walk over to the restaurant when my friend was working. All the food was good, but my favorite thing to eat were these little rolls they served on the bread dish, along with freshly made butter. They were called pecan raisin rolls, and my friend would feed me these babies for free, day after day. She would even smuggle out bags of them, and I would take them home and eat them, one after the other; I was one happy camper. To me, the rolls were sustenance, but they also brought me happiness. Not only did they taste good, but they were from someone I cared about, and who cared that I was well fed. That meant a lot to me.

When I finally figured out, after many tries, how to re-create this beautiful little roll without the gluten, I was hit with a wave of nostalgia. The taste took me back to the days in that tiny little apartment with the rolls from my friend that felt like all I could ever need. Now I share this special recipe with you, and I hope you enjoy it. I often use the bread for sandwiches, as well as French toast. It adds something extra special to anything it touches.

Note that this bread is essentially the same recipe as the Artisan Bread (page 213), except with the addition of the pecans and raisins. This recipe is similarly versatile. You can make it into larger rounds, smaller dinner-size rolls, or long thin baguettes. Or try all three versions—you'll never get tired of this bread.

Raisin Pecan Bread

Makes four 6-inch round loaves

2 cups warm filtered water

1/3 cup olive oil

3 tablespoons raw honey or real maple syrup

2 teaspoons apple cider vinegar

2 tablespoons dry active yeast

1/3 cup chia seeds

1 1/2 cups room-temperature filtered water

2 cups millet flour

1 1/2 cups sorghum flour

1/2 cup brown rice flour

1 1/2 cups tapioca starch

1 1/2 cups potato starch

1 1/2 tablespoons xanthan gum

1 tablespoon Himalayan salt

1 cup chopped pecans

1 cup raisins

Preheat the oven to 400°F. Line a baking sheet with parchment paper.

In a small bowl, whisk together the warm water, olive oil, honey, vinegar, and yeast. Set aside for at least 5 minutes to let the yeast activate. In a separate small bowl, mix the chia seeds with the room-temperature water. Set aside for a few minutes.

—→ recipe continues

Raisin Pecan Bread,
continued

In a stand mixer with the paddle attachment, combine the flours, starches, xanthan gum, and salt. Add the yeast mixture and chia seed mixture and whip on high speed for 2 to 3 minutes, until everything is well combined and smooth. Fold in the pecans and raisins until fully incorporated.

Using your hands, scoop the dough into 4 portions and shape into rounds on the baking sheet. Using a knife, score the top of each loaf with an X. Bake for 40 minutes and check the internal temperature with a meat thermometer. When the bread reaches 200°F, it is done. If it's not up to temperature, keep baking until you've reached 200°F; it is the best sign of doneness. Let cool completely before slicing.

THIS IS a classic Italian bread that I remember from my childhood. I don't think I liked it as a child; the taste was too sophisticated. But sure enough, as an adult, the taste of fennel and golden raisins is perfect. This is one of the recipes that made me do the happy dance in my kitchen when I mastered it. It is crazy-amazing as a sandwich bread for any sandwich in this book or any sandwich you might invent, but it's also fantastic simply toasted and drizzled with olive oil and a sprinkle of sea salt. You will be kissing the tips of your fingers and saying *molto bene* when you try this.

Makes one 10-inch rectangular loaf

Golden Raisin-Fennel Bread

1 tablespoon palm shortening, nondairy butter (such as Earth Balance), or coconut oil, for the pan

5 teaspoons raw honey

3/4 cup warm filtered water

2 1/2 teaspoons active dry yeast

2 teaspoons olive oil, plus more for brushing

2 cups Jennifer's Way Bakery All-Purpose Flour Mix (purchased or page 211)

1 1/2 teaspoons Himalayan salt

1 cup golden raisins

2 teaspoons fennel seeds

Grease a loaf pan with the shortening.

In a small bowl, whisk together 2 teaspoons of the honey, the warm water, and the yeast. Let sit for about 5 minutes to activate the yeast. When the mixture starts to look foamy, add the olive oil and remaining 3 teaspoons honey.

In a stand mixer with the paddle attachment, combine the flour mix and salt. On medium speed, add the yeast mixture, pouring slowly. Mix until combined. Gently fold in the raisins and fennel seeds.

Spoon into the pan, but do not flatten or smooth the top of the dough. Cover with a damp kitchen towel and let the dough rise in a warm place for 30 to 40 minutes. It should be noticeably increased in size.

Preheat the oven to 400°F. Brush the top of the dough with olive oil and, using a sharp knife, score it with a few diagonal slash marks. Bake for 40 to 45 minutes, until it registers an internal temperature of 200°F on a meat thermometer.

Allow to cool completely, slice, and serve or use for sandwiches or crostini. This bread freezes very well, so if you have leftovers, slice and freeze the slices for easy sandwiches or toast.

THIS RECIPE is the bread form of warm and cozy. I created it on a particularly cold, dark, and dreary New York City day. You know those days when you want to just hunker down with a warm blanket, a cup of tea, and a slice of good bread? This is the remedy for those days. I like to make it in the fall, when autumn squashes are at their peak. It isn't very sweet, but it's not savory either. It's somewhere in the middle, which makes it perfect for any meal or snack, especially breakfast. Enjoy plain or toasted, with honey, jam, coconut butter, nut butter, the Honey Butter on page 233—or any butter you can dream up. You could even serve it warm with nondairy ice cream for a dessert treat. To make it even more dessert-like, add 1 cup nondairy chocolate chips to the batter and/or drizzle the top of the loaf with 2 tablespoons real maple syrup before baking. If you like, toast the pecans for a few minutes in a skillet on the stove before adding to the batter to make them even more flavorful. You can also eliminate the nuts if you have an allergy, or want to be kinder to your digestion.

Butternut Squash Bread

Makes 1 loaf

1 medium butternut squash

1 cup Jennifer's Way Bakery All-Purpose Flour Mix (purchased or page 211)

1 cup buckwheat flour

1 teaspoon aluminum-free baking powder

1 teaspoon baking soda

1 tablespoon pumpkin pie spice

1 teaspoon ground cinnamon

½ teaspoon ground ginger

½ teaspoon ground cloves

1 teaspoon Himalayan salt

½ very ripe banana

½ cup real maple syrup

⅓ cup coconut oil or palm shortening

¼ cup plain coconut yogurt (or other nondairy yogurt), no added fruit or sweetener

½ cup full-fat canned coconut milk (or nondairy milk of choice)

⅓ cup chopped pecans

Preheat the oven to 375°F. Line a baking sheet with parchment paper. Line a 9 x 5-inch loaf pan with parchment (or lightly coat it with coconut oil and sprinkle my all-purpose flour or buckwheat flour lightly over the bottom and sides).

Peel the squash and cut it into cubes. (To make this a little easier, first pierce the squash all over and put it in the microwave on high for 5 minutes.) Place the squash on the lined baking sheet and roast until a fork goes through easily, about 40 minutes, depending on how big your cubes are. Set aside to cool.

When cool enough to handle, put the squash in a ziplock bag and squeeze together to mash up. Measure out 1 cup. Refrigerate the remainder to use for another recipe (or just to warm up and eat later for a snack).

In a small bowl, combine all the dry ingredients (through salt) and whisk out any lumps. Using a stand mixer with a paddle attachment, combine the roasted squash, banana, maple syrup, coconut oil, and yogurt. Add the dry ingredients, mixing a little at a time and alternating with the coconut milk. Combine until all the ingredients are mixed well. If the dough seems too dry, add another tablespoon of coconut milk. Fold in the pecans.

Place the dough in the lined loaf pan. Lightly wet your hands with water and smooth out the top of the dough. Bake in the 375°F oven for about 35 minutes, until a toothpick inserted into the center comes out clean. Let the bread cool on a cooling rack for at least 40 minutes.

Indulgent Breakfasts

When I use the word "Indulgent," I am referring to foods that might be more likely to cause inflammation in some people. For example, pancakes made with grains, nuts, and chocolate chips could be inflammatory for you or more difficult to digest. That's why they are in this section. Every recipe here is still a nutritional powerhouse, including the pancakes, which have wonderful fiber and healthy fats. If you find these items don't bother you, then you can enjoy them any time.

MY GRANDFATHER lived in Florida and, when I visited as a child, he would take us for the early bird special at his local diner: two eggs, two pancakes, two sausages, and two pieces of bacon, all for $2.99, if you arrived before 8:00 a.m. We always made it on time, I always ordered chocolate chips in my pancakes, and I always ate every bite. I never forget those pancakes. And then, well...you know the next part. It was good-bye to pancakes for me.

Until now. Honestly, I think that these pancakes are even better than the ones I remember—the pumpkin adds fiber and the chocolate chips add that extra yumminess that I will always crave.

Makes about 6 medium or 12 small pancakes

Pumpkin-Hazelnut-Chocolate Chip Pancakes

½ cup sorghum flour

¼ cup brown rice flour

¼ cup hazelnut flour

½ cup potato starch

¼ teaspoon xanthan gum

1 teaspoon ground cinnamon

½ teaspoon ground or freshly grated nutmeg

½ teaspoon Himalayan salt

1 cup rice milk, coconut milk, or any other additive-free, unsweetened nondairy milk

⅓ cup organic pumpkin purée

2 tablespoons grape seed oil

1½ tablespoons real maple syrup

1 teaspoon ground vanilla bean (or 2 teaspoons gluten-free vanilla extract)

About ½ cup filtered water

Nondairy butter (such as Earth Balance) or additional grape seed oil, for the pan

Dairy-free, naturally sweetened chocolate chips (as many or few as you like)

In a small bowl, combine all the dry ingredients (through salt) using a whisk to get out any lumps.

In a medium bowl, mix together the milk, pumpkin, oil, maple syrup, and vanilla. Slowly mix the dry ingredients into the wet ingredients. Add the water, a little bit at a time, and mix as you go.

Heat a skillet or griddle over medium heat and coat with butter. Spoon or pour 3 or 4 portions of the batter onto the hot skillet or griddle and sprinkle each with a few chocolate chips. Or, make one large pancake at a time. Cook until there are bubbles on the surface of the pancakes (and a few have burst), 1 to 2 minutes. Flip carefully with a spatula, and cook until browned on both sides, 1 to 2 minutes more. Repeat with the remaining batter, adding more butter as needed. Serve and enjoy warm.

THIS WAS the very first recipe I created at my bakery, Jennifer's Way. It was the night before we were due to open our doors and I was beyond nervous and overwhelmed, to say the very least. I had been an actress for 20 years, and now I was opening a bakery with no business experience and no professional baking experience, using only my own personal recipes I made for myself and my friends. What was I thinking! Was I scared? Yeah, you could say that. To calm my jitters, I decided to go to the bakery by myself and quietly bake something special. I remember thinking, "Do something simple, but with a hint of something different. You're a baker now." When these babies started rising in the oven, I knew everything was going to be OK. The scent is pure magic. Warm, inviting, flavorful, and just the confidence boost I needed that night. I hope they can boost your confidence, too, in whatever you dare to do.

Makes 12 muffins

Pear Cardamom Muffins

2 cups Jennifer's Way Bakery All-Purpose Flour Mix (purchased or page 211)

½ cup maple sugar, coconut sugar, date sugar, or evaporated cane juice

1 teaspoon aluminum-free baking powder

1 teaspoon baking soda

1 teaspoon ground cardamom

1 teaspoon ground cinnamon

½ teaspoon Himalayan salt

1 cup puréed peaches, mangoes, or pineapple; or 1 ripe banana, mashed

¼ cup unsweetened applesauce

⅓ cup grape seed oil or olive oil

½ teaspoon ground vanilla bean (or 1 teaspoon gluten-free vanilla extract)

¾ cup rice milk, coconut milk, or any other additive-free, unsweetened nondairy milk

1 pear, peeled, cored, and diced

Preheat the oven to 325°F. Line a standard 12-cup muffin pan with baking liners.

In a medium bowl, whisk together all the dry ingredients (through salt). In a stand mixer with a whisk attachment, combine the fruit purée, applesauce, oil, and vanilla. Set the mixer to medium speed and slowly add the dry ingredients while alternating with the milk. Mix for a minute until everything is incorporated. Remove the bowl from the mixer and slowly fold in the pear.

Scoop the batter into the liners and bake for 10 to 12 minutes, until a toothpick inserted into a muffin comes out clean. Serve immediately, or store into an airtight container in the refrigerator for up to 6 days.

EARLY MORNINGS are not my best time. Something about that alarm ringing in my ear, especially on a Saturday, goes against the natural order for me. When opening my bakery on Saturday mornings, sometimes alone, to get it ready for the day, I have to make *all* the baked items for the day, and this can be overwhelming. So, one morning, having to suddenly become a baker while also not being a morning person, I mistakenly added cocoa powder instead of another kind of flour when making the morning muffins. I am a person who hates to waste anything, so I went with it, and this muffin was born. It's sweet and salty, and the pistachio gives it a unique flavor. That morning, our customers thought I was pretty clever and creative for coming up with such an interesting new morning muffin. I just smiled, knowing it was really just me being half asleep. Happy accidents!

Makes 12 muffins

Chocolate Pistachio Muffins

1 cup Jennifer's Way Bakery All-Purpose Flour Mix (purchased or page 211)

1 cup raw cacao powder or unsweetened organic cocoa powder

1 teaspoon aluminum-free baking powder

1 teaspoon baking soda

½ cup maple sugar, coconut sugar, date sugar, or evaporated cane juice

1 teaspoon ground cinnamon

½ teaspoon Himalayan salt

1 cup shelled, crushed pistachios

1 cup unsweetened applesauce

⅓ cup olive oil

1 teaspoon ground vanilla bean (or 2 teaspoons gluten-free vanilla extract)

¾ cup rice milk, coconut milk, or any other additive-free, unsweetened plant milk

Sea salt to sprinkle on top (optional)

Preheat the oven to 375°F. Line a standard 12-cup muffin pan with baking liners.

In a medium bowl, combine the flour, cacao powder, baking powder, baking soda, sugar, cinnamon, salt, and ½ cup of the pistachios.

Using a stand mixer with the whisk attachment, combine the applesauce, olive oil, and vanilla and mix on medium speed until smooth. Slowly add the dry mix while alternating with the milk.

Scoop the batter into the liners and sprinkle with sea salt (if using) and the rest of the pistachios. Bake for 15 to 20 minutes, until a toothpick inserted into the center of a muffin comes out clean. Muffins will keep in an airtight container in the refrigerator for 3 days.

WHENEVER I make anything that combines orange and vanilla, I hear the bells of the ice cream truck driving too fast down my old block in Brooklyn. When I was a kid, that sound sent chills of joy and excitement right through me. The anticipation of a Creamsicle was almost too much to bear.

This muffin is my homage to the Creamsicle, and also good without the poppy seeds if you are still avoiding seeds. Top with Honey Butter (page 233) for an extra yum factor.

Makes 12 muffins

Orange– Vanilla– Poppy Seed Muffins

2 cups Jennifer's Way Bakery All-Purpose Flour (purchased or page 211)

½ cup maple sugar, coconut sugar, date sugar, or organic evaporated cane juice

1 teaspoon aluminum-free baking powder

1 teaspoon baking soda

1 teaspoon ground cinnamon

½ teaspoon Himalayan salt

2 tablespoons grated orange zest

¾ cup rice milk, coconut milk, or any other additive-free, unsweetened nondairy milk

Juice of ½ orange

½ teaspoon ground vanilla bean or 1 teaspoon gluten-free vanilla extract

1 cup puréed strawberries or peaches (or 1 ripe banana, mashed)

¼ cup unsweetened applesauce

⅓ cup grape seed oil or olive oil

¼ cup poppy seeds

Preheat the oven to 325°F. Line a standard 12-cup muffin pan with baking liners.

In a medium bowl, whisk together the flour, sugar, baking powder, baking soda, cinnamon, salt, and orange zest. In a separate bowl, mix together the milk, orange juice, and vanilla and set aside.

Using a stand mixer with a whisk attachment, combine the fruit purée, applesauce, and oil until smooth. Set the mixer to medium speed and slowly add the dry mixture while alternating with the milk–orange juice mixture. Once everything is added, mix for a minute until everything is incorporated. Remove the bowl from the mixer and fold in the poppy seeds.

Scoop the batter into the liners and bake for 10 to 12 minutes, until a toothpick inserted into a muffin comes out clean.

Serve immediately, or store in an airtight container and refrigerate for up to 6 days.

HONEY AND BUTTER are somehow the perfect combination of flavors. I've always loved both, but I love them even more mixed together. Of course, I can't have real butter anymore, but nondairy butter is a perfectly acceptable substitute. I've also made this with palm shortening, which is surprisingly tasty. I like it on pancakes (page 149), and biscuits (page 69), and toast made from any of my bread recipes. It's also good on the Butternut Squash Bread on page 224.

⟶ *honey butter*

Makes about ¹/₃ cup

⅓ cup palm shortening or nondairy butter (such as Earth Balance)

4 teaspoons olive oil

½ teaspoon fresh lemon juice

½ teaspoon raw honey

¼ teaspoon Himalayan salt, or more to taste

Whip all the ingredients together with a fork (or you could use a hand mixer). Adjust the seasonings to taste. Store in an airtight container in the fridge for honey butter emergencies. It will last for at least 2 weeks.

ONE OF the very first and most popular flavor pairings in our bakery is bananas and chocolate. We always have this recipe in muffin form at the bakery, but I think it's quicker to make in a loaf pan. Still, if you want to make 12 muffins, which are great for putting into school lunches or otherwise taking on-the-go, bake at the same temperature, but for a shorter amount of time: Check with a toothpick after 10 minutes. If it comes out clean, the muffins are done.

Makes 1 loaf (or 12 muffins)

Banana–Chocolate Chip Loaf

1 tablespoon palm shortening, nondairy butter (such as Earth Balance), or coconut oil, for the pan

2 cups Jennifer's Way Bakery All-Purpose Flour Mix (purchased or page 211)

½ cup maple sugar, coconut sugar, date sugar, or evaporated cane juice

1 teaspoon aluminum-free baking powder

1 teaspoon baking soda

1 teaspoon ground cinnamon

½ teaspoon Himalayan salt

2 ripe bananas

⅓ cup grape seed oil or olive oil

¼ cup unsweetened applesauce

1 teaspoon ground vanilla bean (or 2 teaspoons gluten-free vanilla extract)

½ cup canned full-fat coconut milk, unsweetened rice milk, coconut milk, or any other additive-free, unsweetened nondairy milk

¾ cup dairy-free, naturally sweetened chocolate chips

Preheat the oven to 350°F. Grease a loaf pan with the shortening.

In a small bowl, whisk together all the dry ingredients (through salt). Using a stand mixer with a whisk attachment, mix the bananas, oil, applesauce, and vanilla until smooth. Mixing on medium speed, slowly add the dry mixture while alternating with the milk. Once everything is added, mix for an additional minute, until everything is thoroughly incorporated. Fold in the chocolate chips.

Pour the batter into the pan and bake for 15 to 20 minutes, until a toothpick inserted into the center comes out clean. Cool completely, slice, and enjoy plain or with Honey Butter (page 233). Wrapped bread will keep in the refrigerator for about 3 days.

ONE OF MY favorite things to do is sit with a new cookbook, or an old favorite cookbook, and read it from cover to cover. It is like reading a novel. I can seriously get lost for hours. I read every kind of cookbook I can get my hands on, including cookbooks in languages I don't even speak because I like to try to figure out the recipes. I've discovered and learned quite a lot doing this. Even recipes in magazines fascinate me, and this recipe is adapted from one I saw while at a doctor's office, of all places. I remember looking at the recipe quickly, and of course it was loaded with butter and white flour, but the other ingredients made my mouth start watering. Full confession: I decided I needed to "borrow" that magazine from the waiting room and jot down some notes so I could adapt it to something I could eat.

Weeks later, in the bakery, I found a crumpled piece of paper in my purse that said, "Zucchini Hazelnuts Raisins Cranberries Delicious." Really, that was all the help I was going to get from myself? Of course I couldn't find the "borrowed" magazine anywhere, so this was all I had to go on.

Even so, I got to work, and my creation remains one of my favorites to this day. It has an earthy fall flavor and the ingredients, although many and various, work together perfectly. I have served the loaf as a breakfast cake, for lunch, and warmed with dairy-free ice cream after dinner. Sometimes I have a piece with no adornment as a snack. No matter how I enjoy it, I'm always glad I had to wait in that doctor's office that day.

"Zucchini Hazelnut Raisin Cranberry Delicious" Loaf

Makes 1 loaf

1 tablespoon palm shortening, nondairy butter (such as Earth Balance), or coconut oil, for the pan

½ cup crushed or chopped hazelnuts

2 cups Jennifer's Way All-Purpose Flour Mix (purchased or page 211)

½ cup maple sugar, coconut sugar, date sugar, or evaporated cane juice

1 teaspoon aluminum-free baking powder

1 teaspoon baking soda

1 teaspoon ground cinnamon

1 teaspoon ground or freshly grated nutmeg

½ teaspoon Himalayan salt

½ cup unsweetened applesauce

⅓ cup olive oil

1 teaspoon ground vanilla bean (or 2 teaspoons gluten-free vanilla extract)

1½ cups rice milk, coconut milk, or any other additive-free, unsweetened nondairy milk

1 cup shredded zucchini

½ cup raisins

½ cup dried cranberries (look for unsweetened)

Preheat the oven to 350°F. Grease a loaf pan with the shortening and set aside. Line a baking sheet with parchment paper.

Spread the hazelnuts on the lined baking sheet and roast for about 10 minutes, or until fragrant. Set aside to cool.

In a small bowl, whisk together the flour, sugar, baking powder, baking soda, cinnamon, nutmeg, and salt.

In a separate bowl, combine the applesauce, oil, and vanilla. Mix with a hand mixer on high speed until smooth. Set the mixer to medium speed and slowly add the flour mixture while alternating with the milk. Continue mixing until thoroughly combined.

Using a spatula, fold in the hazelnuts, zucchini, raisins, and cranberries. Mix until everything is incorporated.

Pour the batter into the pan and bake for 25 to 30 minutes, until a toothpick inserted into the center comes out clean. Cool completely, slice, and enjoy plain or with Honey Butter (page 233). Wrapped bread will keep in the refrigerator for about 3 days.

Indulgent Sandwiches and Crostini

What better thing to do with bread than make a sandwich? Maybe you thought your sandwich days were over, but with all this great bread, that's just not true. Crostini is another great way to get the sandwich feel, but with half the bread. These are some of my favorite sandwiches and crostini, which I often eat for lunch or snacks, or sometimes as a light dinner.

THIS IS A GROWN-UP, allergen-free version of that kid favorite, the peanut butter–honey–banana sandwich. Instead, this uses sun butter, which is a nice name for sunflower seed butter. Many people who are allergic to nuts and/or peanuts are not allergic to seeds, and so can tolerate sun butter. Try this rich, delicious, lip-smacking sandwich and revel in a meal you can prepare in less than 2 minutes if you already have Raisin Pecan Bread sitting around.

Makes 2 sandwiches

4 slices Raisin Pecan Bread (page 219)

1 banana, sliced

Sun butter

2 tablespoons raw honey

Sun Butter–Honey–Banana Sandwich

Place 2 slices of bread on a plate. Smear as much sun butter as you like on each slice. Arrange the banana slices on the two slices and drizzle each with 1 tablespoon honey. Finish off with a second slice of bread, and enjoy your meal-in-no-time.

THIS SANDWICH tastes like a gourmet treat, but it takes only about a minute to make, so if you don't have much time, you can whip it together and still feel fancy.

Makes 2 sandwiches

4 slices Raisin Pecan Bread (page 219)

½ cup arugula

1 pear, peeled, cored, and sliced

2 tablespoons raw honey

1 tablespoon olive oil

Sea salt

Honey-Pear-Arugula Sandwich

To assemble, place 2 slices of bread on a plate and stack each with the arugula and pear slices, dividing them evenly between the two sandwiches. Drizzle both sandwiches with the honey and olive oil and sprinkle with sea salt. Finish off each with the second slice of bread, and savor every bite.

TOAST BREAD, put something on top of it, give it to me, and I will be in heaven. You can still have crostini, and the sky is the limit in terms of what you put on them. They are great as appetizers for a party, as everyday snacks, or even for breakfast, depending on the topping.

Use this basic recipe to create the base, then try any of the variations that follow, or make up your own. (You can omit the rosemary if it doesn't match your toppings, as in the crostini recipes on pages 242 and 246.) Crostini are always popular at parties: You can double, triple, or further increase the amounts if you are making them for a large group.

Basic Rosemary Crostini

Serves 2 to 4

8 baguette slices or 3- to 5-inch pieces sliced Jennifer's Way Classic Artisan Bread (page 213) or Amazing Grain-Free Artisan Bread (page 99)

2 tablespoons olive oil

1 tablespoon dried rosemary

1 tablespoon Himalayan or kosher salt

Preheat the oven to 450°F. Line a baking sheet with parchment paper.

Arrange the bread on the lined baking sheet and brush the tops with half the olive oil. Toast the bread in the oven for 5 to 8 minutes, until just beginning to turn golden (watch it so it doesn't burn). Remove from the oven, flip, and brush with the remaining olive oil, then sprinkle with the rosemary and salt. Return to the oven and toast for an additional 2 to 3 minutes. The resulting bread should be crisp enough to hold toppings.

ANYTHING on bread makes me happy, but figs and honey are a dream combo in my world. Add some salt and olive oil, and you've got perfection on toast. Added bonus: Using local raw honey from your area may help your immune system fight seasonal allergies.

Fig and Honey Crostini

Serves 2 to 4

5 tablespoons chopped walnuts
5 fresh figs, sliced lengthwise
Basic Rosemary Crostini (page 241)
Drizzle of raw honey
Drizzle of olive oil
Pinch of Himalayan or kosher salt

Preheat the oven to 325°F. Line a baking sheet with parchment paper.

Scatter the walnuts on the lined baking sheet and toast in the oven until fragrant, about 10 minutes.

Place the fig slices on the crostini, then divide the nuts over the figs. Drizzle with the honey and olive oil and sprinkle with salt. Serve immediately.

I FIRST came up with this unique flavor combination for crostini when the bakery was asked to prepare appetizers for a wedding reception. They were a huge hit. You might not have thought of using squash on crostini, but paired with toasty chopped hazelnuts, it works.

Butternut Squash Crostini with Toasted Hazelnuts

Serves 2 to 4

1½ cups cubed peeled butternut squash

1 teaspoon real maple syrup

1 teaspoon chopped fresh or dried sage

½ teaspoon ground cinnamon

3 tablespoons chopped hazelnuts

Basic Rosemary Crostini (page 241)

1 tablespoon olive oil

Pinch of Himalayan salt

Preheat the oven to 400°F. Line 2 baking sheets with parchment paper.

In a large bowl, combine the squash cubes, maple syrup, sage, and cinnamon. Spread on one lined baking sheet and roast until the squash is soft, about 40 minutes.

Meanwhile, spread the chopped hazelnuts on the second lined baking sheet. Toast on a separate rack in the oven until fragrant, 5 to 7 minutes. Let the squash and nuts cool.

When the squash is cool to the touch, place big spoonfuls on the crostini. Gently press down on the squash with a fork to smash it. Sprinkle with the hazelnuts, drizzle with the olive oil, and sprinkle with salt. Serve immediately.

HERE ARE two more of my favorite crostini recipes, one with some fancy cured meat (which I try not to eat too often), and another with luscious (but sometimes acidifying) fresh tomatoes. They are both simple to assemble, whether you want to impress your guests, or just yourself.

Prosciutto-Pear Crostini

Serves 2 to 4

Basic Rosemary Crostini
(page 241), rosemary omitted

8 slices prosciutto

1 tablespoon olive oil, plus more
to drizzle

2 Bartlett pears, cut into quarters
and cored

Drizzle of raw honey

Pinch of Himalayan or kosher salt

Set the crostini on a plate or platter and top each with a slice of prosciutto.

In a skillet, heat the olive oil over medium heat. Place the pear quarters in the skillet and cook until a fork goes in easily but they are not mushy, about 5 minutes.

Top each prosciutto slice with a sautéed pear quarter. Drizzle with honey and more olive oil, and sprinkle with salt. Serve immediately.

Tomato–Basil Crostini

Basic Rosemary Crostini
(page 241), rosemary omitted

3 medium tomatoes, cut into
16 slices

8 fresh basil leaves with stems
torn off

Drizzle of olive oil

Pinch of Himalayan or kosher salt

Pinch of freshly ground
black pepper

Set the prepared crostini on a plate or platter and top each with
2 tomato slices. Place a basil leaf on top of each. Drizzle with
olive oil and sprinkle with salt and pepper. Serve immediately.

Indulgent Meals, Pasta, and Potatoes

Whether a beautiful organic piece of meat or a plate of savory pasta, my Indulgent meals can be elegant dinners for just you (with jealousy-inducing leftovers) or can feed your family or friends. They are all good for dinner parties too. Nobody will suspect they are being well nourished.

STICKY FINGERS covered in barbecue sauce that you absolutely must lick is pretty much synonymous with summer for me, in the best possible way. I make this BBQ sauce every year, keeping it in the refrigerator in large sealed plastic bags, just waiting for some ribs to smother in it. While there are many barbecue sauces out there on store shelves, most have hidden ingredients many of us can't have, not to mention tons of sodium and sugar that we certainly don't need. My sauce boasts all the wonderful flavors you remember, but is made in a way you can enjoy without worry or reaction. You can easily double or triple the sauce if you need more, or want to make the sauce ahead and keep handy.

Here is my favorite way to use the sauce, on baby back ribs from the organic butcher, but I also love a good grilled chicken. (To grill bone-in chicken pieces or boneless chicken breasts, cook on high heat with the top closed for approximately 25 minutes or until the inside is no longer pink, basting with the sauce during the last 10 minutes.) But if you are a fan of ribs, you will love this recipe...and if you cook them on the grill, you may have a small crowd gathering, waiting for them to be done. Enjoy, and feel free to lick those fingers!

Serves 2 to 4, depending on how hungry you are

2 tablespoons olive oil
2 shallots, minced
2 cloves garlic, minced
¼ cup molasses
¼ cup organic tomato paste
2 tablespoons raw honey
4 teaspoons apple cider vinegar
1½ teaspoons tamari
1 teaspoon paprika
1 teaspoon ground turmeric
½ teaspoon cayenne pepper
Pinch of Himalayan salt
1 rack baby back ribs

Jennifer's Famous BBQ Baby Back Ribs

Coat a medium saucepan with the oil and heat over medium heat. Add the shallots and garlic and cook until translucent. Add the molasses, tomato paste, honey, vinegar, tamari, paprika, turmeric, cayenne, and salt. Cook until the sauce just begins to bubble. Reduce the heat and simmer on low for 10 minutes. Let cool completely. (Makes about ¾ cup barbecue sauce.)

Put your baby back ribs in a large ziplock bag. Pour ½ cup of the sauce into the bag, seal it, and move it around to completely coat the ribs. Let them marinate in the refrigerator for no less than 3 hours, or up to 24 hours.

Set up an outdoor grill for low heat. Remove the ribs from the bag and grill over the low fire for a couple of hours, or until the meat is tender and falling off the bone, brushing with the remaining BBQ sauce during the last 5 minutes of cooking.

GRILLED PEACHES

As long as you've got the grill fired up, you might as well use it to make dessert. Grilled fruit is amazing. If you've never tried it, this is your chance, especially in the summer when peaches are at their ripe, juicy peak. The maple glaze takes fresh peaches to the next level, while the chocolate, hazelnuts, and sea salt are almost too much to take...*almost*. Try serving with some nondairy coconut ice cream for a perfect end to a summer night.

Note that although this recipe is in the Indulgent section because it can be grilled while making some of other recipes here, it is completely and utterly okay to eat, even when you are eating Pure. If you leave off the hazelnuts and use unsweetened chocolate, there will be nothing in this recipe to inflame you, so I hope you will enjoy it often. You could also make it in the broiler if you crave it but don't want to start up the grill. Just watch the peaches carefully. They may only need to be broiled for 5 minutes on each side.

Grilled Maple-Glazed Peaches with Chocolate Drizzle

Serves 2 (can easily be doubled or tripled)

¼ cup real maple syrup

1 teaspoon ground cinnamon

2 peaches, cut in half, pits removed

2 tablespoons raw cacao nibs, nondairy naturally sweetened chocolate chips, or broken-up chunks of your favorite raw chocolate bar

1 teaspoon nondairy butter (such as Earth Balance)

2 tablespoons chopped hazelnuts

Pinch of sea salt (or Himalayan or kosher salt)

In a small bowl, combine the maple syrup and cinnamon. Place the peaches on a plate and brush the maple glaze on both sides. Grill on an outside grill over a medium fire, or indoors on a grill pan over medium heat, for about 10 minutes on each side. The peaches should be soft but not mushy. Transfer to a serving dish and let cool.

In a double boiler or a heat-safe bowl sitting on top of a saucepan filled with simmering water, melt the cacao nibs and butter together, stirring constantly until smooth (this could take 10 minutes or so). With a spoon, drizzle the peaches with the warm chocolate mixture. Sprinkle with the crushed hazelnuts and salt.

HOLY MOLEY, this baby is good! I created this recipe after watching Martha Stewart make lasagna on her show a long time ago. I was determined to make something as rich and delicious, just without the dairy. Sadly, ricotta cheese seemed to be essential for a real lasagna, and I couldn't figure out how to make a dairy-free version. I'd seen some vegan versions made with nuts, but I couldn't digest them. I needed a substitute, so I started to think of what might make a creamy center. Then I had an inspiration: My old friend the butternut squash could stand in for the ricotta cheese! And then, why not use my other secret weapon, the chameleon known as the cauliflower, to re-create the béchamel sauce? Now I was really onto something.

I'm warning you now, this recipe has a lot of steps. That's one of the reasons I put it in the Indulgent section—you need to be feeling pretty good and have high energy to take on this project— but holy ricotta, it is worth every second of prep and cook time! It is an indulgent special-occasion meal meant to be shared with friends and family. You'll blow them away.

You could add a little cooked chopped or ground organic turkey, chicken, or grass-fed beef on top of the squash layer if you want it to contain more protein.

Serves 8

Roasted Butternut Squash Lasagna

2 large butternut squashes

2 tablespoons olive oil

1 teaspoon Himalayan salt, plus more to taste

1 teaspoon freshly ground black pepper

2 (9- or 10-ounce) boxes gluten-free lasagna noodles

¾ cup almond milk

½ cup nondairy butter (such as Earth Balance)

¼ cup finely chopped hazelnuts

¼ cup chopped fresh sage leaves

1 teaspoon ground nutmeg

BÉCHAMEL

¼ cup olive oil

½ cup minced yellow onion

3 cups cauliflower florets

1 cup filtered water

1¾ cups almond milk

6 tablespoons nondairy butter (such as Earth Balance)

3 tablespoons tapioca starch

1 teaspoon ground or freshly grated nutmeg, plus more for sprinkling

½ teaspoon kosher salt

Preheat the oven to 400°F.

Cut the squashes in half lengthwise and remove the seeds (if you prick them all over with a fork and microwave for 5 minutes,

⟶ recipe continues

this is easier to do). Drizzle the cut sides with the olive oil, salt, and pepper. Place cut sides down on a baking sheet and roast for about 1 hour, until nicely browned and soft. You should be able to put a fork through the skin. Let cool, then scoop out the flesh from the skins and purée in a food processor until completely smooth. Leave in the food processor.

While the squashes are in the oven, cook the lasagna noodles according to the package directions. Drain, rinse, and set aside.

While the pasta is cooking, in a saucepan over low heat, combine the almond milk, butter, hazelnuts, sage, and nutmeg. Heat and stir until smooth, then add more salt to taste. Add this mixture to the butternut squash and process until fully combined. Put the squash mixture in a bowl and set aside. Rinse out the food processor so you can use it for the béchamel sauce.

FOR THE BÉCHAMEL: Rinse out the saucepan, add 2 tablespoons of the olive oil, and heat over medium heat. Add the onion and cook until translucent. Add the cauliflower and cook and stir for 2 minutes, then add the water. Cover and cook until the cauliflower is soft, about 10 minutes. Transfer the mixture to the food processor and process until puréed. Leave in the food processor.

Rinse out the saucepan again and add the almond milk, butter, tapioca starch, nutmeg, and salt. Stir or whisk for 2 to 3 minutes over low heat, until smooth. Add to the cauliflower purée in the food processor and process until everything is combined, adding the remaining 2 tablespoons olive oil as you process.

ASSEMBLE THE LASAGNA: Ladle a small amount of béchamel into a 9 x 12-inch baking dish with high sides, just enough to cover the bottom with a thin layer. Next, cover the bottom with lasagna noodles. Spread with half the butternut squash mixture.

Make a second layer of the béchamel, noodles, and squash. End with another layer of noodles covered with the last of the béchamel sauce and sprinkled with nutmeg.

Lower the oven temperature to 375°F. Cover the lasagna with foil and bake for 20 minutes. Take off the foil and bake uncovered for 35 more minutes, or until the lasagna is bubbling gently. Remove from the oven and let the lasagna sit for about 10 minutes, then cut into squares and serve with crusty bread of your choice. Enjoy!

IN MANHATTAN'S EAST VILLAGE there is a restaurant called Frank that my friends and I used to frequent. It had the best Italian food you could imagine, at amazing prices. The restaurant started with only ten tables, and became a favorite from word of mouth. In those days, the young owner, who became a friend, had four other restaurants as well. Basically, his secret was to take his grandmother's recipes and create the simplest dishes using only the very best and freshest ingredients. One night, my friends and I ran into the chef and he invited us all back to his closed restaurant. It was 3 a.m. (I definitely can't do those kinds of late nights anymore, but those were the days.) Anyway, he said he would make us something simple: pasta with lemon and Parmesan. I instantly grimaced. Lemon on pasta? But he went into the back and in what seemed like minutes, he reappeared with a piping-hot bowl of pasta tossed with Parmesan cheese, olive oil, and lemon and topped with fresh parsley. Tentatively, I tried it. Shock and awe. I didn't just like it, I was mad for it. I had never imagined those flavors could ever add so many dimensions to a simple pasta.

Through the years, I re-created the pasta many times, and people often asked me for the recipe because they loved it so much. Then celiac came along, and there I was, stuck with new rules: no pasta, no cheese. I figured out that I could substitute the pasta, as there are now many high-quality, great-tasting gluten-free pastas out there. But cheese? Italian Parmesan? Sorry, but that is a big fat *no*. I'd heard of nut cheese, but I can't handle nuts very well either and it sounded terrible. I had to think of some other ingenious way to re-create the flavor of that pasta.

Then I discovered seaweed gomasio, a Japanese seasoning consisting of sesame seeds, salt, and seaweed. Amazingly, when combined with hot pasta, it becomes a starchy, savory substitute for Parmesan cheese! So I gave it a try with lemon and pasta. A hit! I have made this many times since and, to tell the truth, I will *always* miss Parmesan cheese—but this version still hits the spot.

You may be able to find seaweed gomasio in your local health food store, but you can definitely buy it online. Eden Organic makes a good version.

Lemon Sesame Spaghetti

Serves 6

Himalayan salt
1 pound gluten-free spaghetti
2 tablespoons seaweed gomasio
2 tablespoons olive oil
Grated zest of 1 lemon
Juice of ½ lemon
Freshly ground black pepper

Fill a medium to large saucepan with water, sprinkle in some salt, and bring to a boil for the pasta. Cook the spaghetti according to the package instructions until al dente. Drain and return to the warm saucepan. Add the gomasio, olive oil, and lemon zest and juice. Season with salt and pepper, mix to combine, and serve hot.

MY GRANDMOTHER used to make Bolognese and let it simmer for hours. When I make it, I've done it that way, but I've also cooked it much more quickly. Honestly, either way, it's crazy good. It's one of my favorite things to make on a Sunday, then serve up with a fresh-baked loaf of bread to soak up all the sauce and meat. This can feed a few people or many, and the sauce freezes really well, so you can have batches of it ready to go for the nights when all you have the energy to do is boil some pasta.

Serves 6

Classic Pasta Bolognese

2 tablespoons olive oil, plus more for serving

1 small yellow onion, coarsely chopped

2 cloves garlic, minced

1 small carrot, chopped

1 stalk celery, minced

1 pound ground turkey or beef, preferably organic and, if using beef, grass fed

1 (15-ounce) can organic crushed tomatoes

1 teaspoon Himalayan salt, plus more to taste

Red pepper flakes (optional)

1 (12-ounce) package gluten-free pasta, any shape

½ cup chopped fresh Italian parsley

Freshly ground black pepper

In a large saucepan, heat the olive oil over medium-high heat. Add the onion and cook until translucent. Stir in the garlic and continue to cook for 1 minute. Add the carrot and celery and cook, stirring as you go, until soft, another 5 minutes. Add the meat and cook until browned.

When the meat is cooked through, add the tomatoes and salt, turn the heat down to low, and let simmer for about 30 minutes. Stir in the red pepper flakes if using.

While the sauce is simmering, fill a medium to large saucepan with water, sprinkle in some salt, and bring to a boil for the pasta. Cook the pasta according to the package directions.

Drain the pasta and return to the warm saucepan. Add the sauce and toss to coat. Top with parsley, a drizzle of olive oil, and additional salt and pepper to taste.

Store leftover pasta/sauce in the refrigerator for up to 3 days, or in the freezer for up to 3 months.

I ONCE TOLD a room full of Italians that my secret meatball ingredient was applesauce. I got a three-pronged response: gasps, a tense silence, and then a heated debate between aunts and uncles. Who makes meatballs with applesauce? Apparently, I do.

Well, when you can't have eggs and you want real Sunday meatballs, then you have one choice: Figure it out. So I did—and it turns out applesauce does the trick of binding the meatballs, and no one would have been the wiser if I hadn't admitted it. Lesson learned: If your big Italian family is happily eating, go ahead and keep your applesauce secrets to yourself.

I include this recipe in the pasta section because meatballs are often added to a nice marinara sauce (if you have one you already like to make), and you could add them to the Classic Spaghetti Bolognese recipe instead of the ground meat (make the sauce without the meat and stir in the meatballs at the end). However, a very popular way to eat these meatballs is on their own, with pasta on the side, so try them however you like. They are good in or out of the sauce.

Serves 6

1½ pounds ground beef (organic grass fed preferable)

1 small yellow onion, minced

3 cloves garlic, minced

¼ cup unsweetened applesauce

1 tablespoon chopped fresh Italian parsley

½ teaspoon garlic salt

2 teaspoons Himalayan salt

1 teaspoon freshly ground black pepper

2 teaspoons olive oil

Italian-Style Meatballs

Combine the beef, onion, garlic, applesauce, parsley, garlic salt, Himalayan salt, and pepper in a large bowl. Mix gently with your hands until just combined. Do not overmix or your meatballs will be tough. Take large spoonfuls and roll between your palms to form into 1-inch balls. Set on a plate near the stove.

Coat a frying pan or cast-iron skillet with the olive oil and heat over medium-high heat until a drop of water in the skillet sizzles. Place the meatballs in the pan, in batches if they are crowded, and cook, turning frequently, until browned on all sides. Lower the heat, cover, and cook for about 10 minutes. Check the meatballs to be sure they are cooked through and there is no pink remaining.

Store leftover meatballs in an airtight container in the refrigerator for up to 4 days, or freeze for up to a month.

OH BOY, does this recipe bring out the kid in me! I don't know if it's the marshmallows or the whipped sweet potatoes or the memories of my sister and me picking the crunchy melted marshmallows off the top. But whatever it is, Thanksgiving isn't Thanksgiving to me without marshmallowed sweet potatoes. Just make sure when buying your marshmallows that you check the ingredients label carefully. You can get natural marshmallows at health food stores, but regular brands will work too. Just keep in mind that they do contain refined sugar, so this is really a once-or-twice-a-year kind of recipe. However, if you're definitely anti-marshmallow, the sweet potatoes are actually pretty good even without the happy marshmallow topping.

Mashed Sweet Potatoes with Marshmallows

Serves 8

5 sweet potatoes, peeled and cubed

½ cup nondairy butter (such as Earth Balance)

2 tablespoons full-fat canned coconut milk

2 tablespoons real maple syrup

2 tablespoons ground cinnamon

1 teaspoon ground or freshly grated nutmeg

½ teaspoon ground vanilla bean (or 1 teaspoon gluten-free vanilla extract)

1 teaspoon Himalayan salt

Enough mini marshmallows to cover the top of the potatoes—about 2 cups, more or less (make sure they are gluten free)

Put the sweet potatoes in a large pot and cover with cool water. Bring to a boil over high heat. Reduce the heat and simmer until tender enough to stick a fork in the potatoes easily, 15 to 20 minutes. Drain in a colander and return to the pot.

Add the butter, milk, maple syrup, cinnamon, nutmeg, vanilla, and salt. Beat with a hand mixer until smooth. If the mixture seems too dry, add more coconut milk.

Transfer the sweet potato mixture to a 9 x 13-inch baking dish. Completely cover the top with a single layer of marshmallows so you can't see any potatoes underneath.

Turn on the broiler. Put the sweet potatoes under the broiler and watch carefully. Remove as soon as the marshmallows start to turn golden-brown. Do not leave for even 1 minute longer or they will burn. The whole broiling process will only take a couple of minutes.

Serve warm and enjoy the trip down memory lane!

THANKSGIVING TIME has a particular, wonderfully nostalgic smell—to me, it's of my grandmother's kitchen when she was making amazing stuffing at the stove. My grandmother was a very thin, petite woman who always had stomach issues. I often think about her, and knowing all I know now about celiac disease, I'm convinced that she had it too, but just didn't have a name for it and was never diagnosed.

I offer you this wonderful recipe, modified just slightly from her original to take out the gluten. It still has the same comforting taste that she brought to the table every year. I dedicate this recipe to my grandmother, and hope that when you make the stuffing for your family you enjoy it as much as we did.

Grandma's Thanksgiving Sausage Stuffing

Makes about 8 cups, or 8 servings

2 tablespoons olive oil

1 medium yellow onion, chopped

2 carrots, chopped

5 stalks celery, chopped

1½ pounds ground beef

1½ pounds ground pasture-raised pork

3 cups fresh white mushrooms, chopped

2 tablespoons chopped fresh thyme

2 cups Bone Broth (page 73) or gluten-free chicken broth

4 cups Gluten-Free Croutons (page 218)

1 medium shallot, minced

Himalayan salt

Freshly ground black pepper

Heat the oil in a large skillet over medium heat. Add the onion and cook until translucent, about 5 minutes. Add the carrots and celery and continue cooking for another 5 minutes.

Mix together the beef and pork and add to the pan along with the mushrooms and thyme. Cook until the meat is browned and no longer pink. Add the broth and croutons and mix gently to combine. Turn the heat to low and cook until the croutons are soft, about 8 minutes. Add the shallot, season with salt and pepper, and stir to combine everything. Let sit for 15 minutes to allow the flavors to meld.

Use the stuffing to stuff your Thanksgiving turkey, or bake it separately in a covered casserole dish or baking dish at 350°F for 1 hour. You can also put it in the slow cooker if the turkey is taking up the oven space and cook on low for 4 to 6 hours.

Indulgent Cookies and Cakes

I never know when I might want something sweetly indulgent. It might be for an afternoon snack, when I need a cookie or a slice of a sweet loaf of something. It might be for dessert, when I want something fancy, like a cake, or something simple, like chocolate. Or it might be for a celebration—a birthday, a holiday, or whatever excuse I can come up with to celebrate something. Whatever the holiday, you will be ready to celebrate with these recipes!

THIS IS one of the most famous cookies from my bakery. Not only are they pretty to look at, but they taste incredible. I was inspired to make the cookies because of Brooklyn. Growing up, there seemed to be an Italian bakery on every corner, and our corner was no exception. I used to practically float down the street on the power of the aroma alone, drawing me to my favorite spot where I would buy the cookies, which were not only filled with jam but also dipped in melted chocolate. (You could do that too, after they've cooled.) Hazelnut flour makes them nutty and so moist. The fresh jam sends the cookies into the top three favorites of mine.

Makes 12 to 18 cookies

1¾ cups Jennifer's Way Bakery All-Purpose Flour Mix (purchased or page 211)

2 cups hazelnut flour or almond meal flour

½ cup arrowroot starch

1 teaspoon aluminum-free baking powder

½ teaspoon baking soda

¾ teaspoon Himalayan salt

¾ cup palm shortening

½ cup olive oil or grape seed oil

1 cup rice milk, coconut milk, or any other additive-free, unsweetened nondairy milk

About 2 tablespoons jam of choice

Jam Dot Cookies

Using a stand mixer with a whisk attachment, mix the dry ingredients (through salt) until just combined. In a small bowl, combine the shortening and oil, then add to the dry ingredients a few spoonfuls at a time, alternating with ¼ cup of the milk each time, until combined. Refrigerate the dough for at least half an hour, or overnight.

Preheat the oven to 375°F. Line a baking sheet with parchment paper.

Scoop spoonfuls of the dough onto the lined baking sheet. Press each cookie using your thumb to make an indentation. Add ½ teaspoon of the jam to each indentation. Bake for 15 to 20 minutes, until the cookies are just beginning to color. Cool on a wire rack. Store in an airtight container for up to 5 days.

I ONCE READ about a cookie made using savory herbs, and thought, "No way, not for me." Then one afternoon at the bakery, we decided to try something different, and we gave it a go. We haven't looked back since—the rosemary pairs perfectly with the refreshing orange. Now I'm always trying to figure out clever ways to sneak herbs into my desserts. The first rule when venturing into this new way of baking: Throw out the old rules and open your mind to new ideas!

Makes about 12 cookies

Orange-Rosemary Cookies with Orange Glaze

Note: The recipe contains sweet rice flour which is different than regular rice flour. It's made from so-called "sticky rice." Bob's Red Mill is one brand that is relatively easy to find.

1½ cups Jennifer's Way Bakery All-Purpose Flour Mix (purchased or page 211)

¾ cup evaporated cane juice sugar

¼ cup sweet rice flour

¼ teaspoon aluminum-free baking powder

¼ teaspoon baking soda

Grated zest of 1 orange, plus more for garnish

1 tablespoon minced fresh rosemary, plus more for garnish (optional)

¼ teaspoon Himalayan salt

7 tablespoons nondairy butter (such as Earth Balance) or palm shortening

¼ cup unsweetened applesauce

½ cup full-fat canned coconut milk, rice milk, coconut milk, or any other additive-free, unsweetened nondairy milk, mixed with a splash of apple cider vinegar

¼ cup Homemade Powdered Sugar (page 282)

2 tablespoons fresh orange juice

In a medium bowl, combine all the dry ingredients (through salt). Using a stand mixer with a paddle attachment, combine the butter and applesauce and mix on medium speed until smooth. Slowly add the dry ingredients to the wet, a little bit at a time, alternating with the milk. Turn the mixer up to high speed and whip until fluffy. Refrigerate for at least 1 hour.

Preheat the oven to 325°F. Line a baking sheet with parchment paper.

Scoop tablespoonfuls of the chilled cookie dough onto the lined baking sheet and bake for 15 to 20 minutes, until firm. Let cool.

To make the glaze, whisk the powdered sugar with the orange juice until smooth.

Once the cookies have cooled, drizzle with the orange glaze and sprinkle additional rosemary on top (if using). These cookies will keep wrapped in the refrigerator for about 3 days.

I'VE REALLY never had a snickerdoodle in its original form. This cookie came about after I wrote a blog post called "What Do You Miss?" A woman wrote to me about snickerdoodles—a cookie that she used to eat with her beloved grandmother when she was a child. The woman's grandmother had passed along with her snickerdoodle tradition, since she'd been recently diagnosed with celiac disease. I immediately started researching snickerdoodle recipes and enlisted a friend who knew the original taste. Within days we had it: a gluten-free snickerdoodle that would make Nana proud.

Snickerdoodles

Makes 2 dozen cookies

1 cup Jennifer's Way Bakery All-Purpose Flour Mix (purchased or page 211)

⅓ cup maple sugar, coconut sugar, date sugar, or evaporated cane juice

1 teaspoon aluminum-free baking powder

½ teaspoon ground cinnamon

Pinch of Himalayan salt

1 cup unsweetened applesauce

¼ cup palm shortening or nondairy butter (such as Earth Balance)

2 tablespoons real maple syrup

1 tablespoon fresh lemon juice

1 teaspoon ground vanilla bean (or 2 teaspoons gluten-free vanilla extract)

2 tablespoons maple sugar (or date or coconut sugar) mixed with 2 tablespoons ground cinnamon

Combine all the dry ingredients (through salt) in a small bowl and set aside.

In a large bowl, combine the applesauce and shortening. Whip on high speed with a hand mixer (or in a stand mixer with a whisk attachment) until light and fluffy and fully combined. Add the maple syrup, lemon juice, and vanilla and mix at medium speed until incorporated. A little at a time, add the dry ingredients to the wet, mixing between each addition, until completely combined. Cover the bowl with plastic wrap and refrigerate for 1 hour.

Preheat the oven to 375°F. Line 2 baking sheets with parchment paper (or bake in 2 batches). Scoop out a tablespoonful of dough and roll between your palms to create a ball. Set on the lined baking sheet and flatten with a fork. Repeat with the remaining dough. Sprinkle the cookies with the cinnamon sugar and bake for 10 to 12 minutes, until just firm (or longer if you prefer a crispier cookie).

Cool on a wire rack and store any leftover cookies in an airtight container for up to 3 days.

I WAS NEVER allowed to eat the store-bought version of these cupcakes when I was a kid. That is, unless I broke open my piggy bank and snuck to the store on my own to buy a package of the tasty treats. There was just something so enticing about the two perfect chocolate cupcakes in the little clear plastic wrapper.

Now I can just make them in my kitchen—no broken piggy banks necessary! These cupcakes fly off the shelves at the bakery and this is the one recipe my friends are most likely to ask me to make for them. The hidden creamy filling lends a light touch to the rich chocolate cake and the chocolate ganache on top is perfection. Of course, I haven't forgotten the white frosting squiggle! (You can also make this as an entire cake if you want to go large!)

Makes 12 cupcakes

Fauxstess Cupcakes

Note: I almost always give multiple sweetener options in my recipes, but for this particular cake the evaporated cane juice really is the best choice for the most authentic taste.

CUPCAKES

2½ cups Jennifer's Way Bakery All-Purpose Flour Mix (purchased or page 211)

1¼ cups organic unsweetened cocoa powder

2 teaspoons aluminum-free baking powder

2½ teaspoons baking soda

1 cup evaporated cane juice

¼ teaspoon espresso powder

1¼ teaspoons Himalayan salt

1 ripe banana, peeled and mashed

1 cup unsweetened applesauce

¾ cup olive oil

1 cup real maple syrup

1 teaspoon ground vanilla bean (or 2 teaspoons gluten-free vanilla extract)

1¼ cups rice milk, coconut milk, or any other additive-free, unsweetened nondairy milk

CREAM FILLING

1½ cups palm shortening

¾ cup Homemade Powdered Sugar (page 282)

1 teaspoon fresh lemon juice

¼ teaspoon ground vanilla bean (or ½ teaspoon gluten-free vanilla extract)

CHOCOLATE GANACHE

2 cups dairy-free naturally sweetened chocolate chips

½ cup rice milk, coconut milk, or any other additive-free, unsweetened nondairy milk

FOR THE CUPCAKES: Preheat the oven to 350°F. Line a standard 12-cup muffin pan with baking liners (or grease an 8-inch round cake pan with a little bit of palm shortening).

Combine all the dry ingredients (through salt) in a medium bowl and set aside. Using a stand mixer with a whisk attachment,

—→ recipe continues

combine the banana, applesauce, olive oil, maple syrup, and vanilla until smooth. Slowly add the dry mix to the wet, alternating with the milk. Mix on medium speed until a pudding-like consistency.

Scoop the batter into the liners (or cake pan) and bake for 12 to 15 minutes for cupcakes or 20 to 25 minutes for cake, until a toothpick inserted into the center comes out clean. Let cool completely before filling or frosting.

FOR THE CREAM FILLING: Using a stand mixer with a whisk attachment, whip the shortening at a high speed until fluffy. Reduce to medium speed and slowly add the powdered sugar, lemon juice, and vanilla and mix until fluffy. Set aside.

Once the cupcakes have cooled, make a hole in the center of each using the back of a wooden spoon. Put the cream filling in a ziplock bag, and snip off one small corner. Stick the open corner into the hole and fill the center with the cream filling. Reserve enough cream to decorate the top of the cupcakes. Refrigerate the cupcakes for 10 minutes. (If you are making a cake, cool completely. Slice in half horizontally to make 2 layers and fill with the cream filling, reserving some for the top.)

FOR THE CHOCOLATE GANACHE: Combine the chocolate chips and milk in a microwave-safe bowl and microwave at 25-second intervals, stirring between each, until the chocolate is smooth and no lumps are visible.

Dip the tops of the chilled cupcakes into the warm ganache, and place on a baking sheet. Once all cupcakes are frosted, refrigerate for an additional 10 minutes or until the ganache has set. (If you are making a whole cake, just frost it with the ganache and chill until set.)

Decorate with the remaining cream, making a looped line down the center of each cupcake top (or the cake top) to look just like this cupcake's famous predecessor.

THESE HAVE a similar flavor profile to the Orange–Vanilla–Poppy Seed muffins at the beginning of this chapter (page 232), but the cupcake version is complete with frosting! Cupcakes are great for kids and special occasions, but these beauties, sweetened with only antioxidant-rich maple syrup and flavored with a surprise cupcake ingredient (turmeric), are anti-inflammatory, which you don't often see in a cupcake. Of course, no kid will be wiser unless you spill the beans. But anyone can delight in this flavor combination, whether a kid or just a kid at heart. They are light, simple, perfect, and won't slow you down.

Makes 6 cupcakes

Orange–Vanilla Cupcakes

1¾ cups Jennifer's Way Bakery All-Purpose Flour Mix (purchased or page 211)

½ cup maple sugar, coconut sugar, date sugar, or evaporated cane juice

1 teaspoon aluminum-free baking powder

1 teaspoon baking soda

1 teaspoon ground cinnamon

½ teaspoon Himalayan salt

¼ cup unsweetened applesauce

1 ripe banana, peeled and mashed

Juice of 1 orange

⅓ cup coconut flour

¾ cup rice milk, coconut milk, or any other additive-free, unsweetened nondairy milk

Vegan Buttercream (page 285)

Orange zest, to decorate (optional)

Preheat the oven to 350°F. Line a standard 6-cup muffin tin with baking liners.

In a small bowl, whisk together the flour, sugar, baking powder, baking soda, cinnamon, and salt.

In a separate bowl, combine the applesauce, banana, orange juice, and coconut flour and mix with a hand mixer on high speed until smooth. Set the mixer to medium speed, and slowly add the flour mixture while alternating with the milk. Continue mixing until thoroughly combined.

Scoop the batter into the liners. Bake the cupcakes for 10 to 12 minutes, until a toothpick inserted into the center of one comes out clean. Let cool. Frost with the buttercream and garnish with orange zest if you like. Store leftovers in an airtight container for up to 3 days.

I MADE THIS CAKE on my birthday a few years ago. I started with a chocolate cake and then kept adding all of my favorite toppings. Pecans, great! Pecans, coconut, and salt...even better! There is something about mixing salty and sweet that I adore. You can make this as a large Bundt cake to share, or you can make minis if you have a mini Bundt cake pan you want to try out. Happy birthday to you!

Makes one 10-inch Bundt cake or 12 mini Bundt cakes

Chocolate Bundt Cake with Pecans, Coconut, and Himalayan Salt

¾ cup olive oil, plus more for the pan

2½ cups Jennifer's Way Bakery All-Purpose Flour Mix (purchased or page 211)

2 teaspoons aluminum-free baking powder

2½ teaspoons baking soda

1¼ cups organic unsweetened cocoa powder

1 cup maple sugar, coconut sugar, date sugar, or evaporated cane juice

¼ teaspoon espresso powder

1 teaspoon ground vanilla bean (or 2 teaspoons gluten-free vanilla extract)

1¼ teaspoons Himalayan salt

1 ripe banana, peeled and mashed

1 cup unsweetened applesauce

1 cup real maple syrup

1¼ cups rice milk, coconut milk, or any other additive-free, unsweetened nondairy milk

1½ cups crushed pecans

2 cups unsweetened shredded coconut

Kosher salt

Preheat the oven to 350°F. Grease a Bundt cake pan with olive oil.

In a medium bowl, combine the flour, baking powder, baking soda, cocoa, sugar, espresso, vanilla, and Himalayan salt.

Using a stand mixer with a whisk attachment, combine the banana, applesauce, maple syrup, and olive oil until smooth. Slowly add the dry mix alternating with the milk. Mix on medium speed until it has a pudding-like consistency. Fold in 1 cup of the pecans and 1 cup of the coconut.

Sprinkle the remaining ½ cup pecans, remaining 1 cup coconut, and kosher salt on the bottom of the Bundt pan, or divide among the mini Bundt pans. Scoop the batter into the pan(s) and bake for 30 to 35 minutes for a whole cake or 15 to 20 minutes for mini cakes, until a toothpick inserted into the center comes out clean. Cool for 10 to 15 minutes and turn the cake(s) out onto a flat surface. Serve and enjoy warm or at room temperature.

THE CLASSIC fall flavors of pear and cardamom will transport you to crisp nights by a fire. I bake this cake when that urge to turn on the heat and cuddle up kicks in. The taste will transport you, but I have to admit that it's the orange glaze that takes the cake to the next level. You'll be licking your fingers (and the spoon)—I promise. Serve with a warm cup of chamomile tea with honey for even more cozy deliciousness.

There are only a couple of recipes in this book that call for powdered sugar. This is a refined product, even when organic, but it is the perfect ingredient for a glaze, so I figured out how to make my own using tapioca starch and organic evaporated cane juice (see page 282). However, if you definitely want to avoid all cane sugar, you could substitute raw honey for the powdered sugar when making the glaze. It won't be quite the same, but it will still taste good.

Note that you can also make this recipe in 4 mini Bundt pans for individual portions—just remember to check for doneness after 20 minutes.

Serves 8 to 12

Cardamom–Pear Cake with Orange Glaze

1 tablespoon palm shortening, nondairy butter (such as Earth Balance), or coconut oil, for the pan

2 cups Jennifer's Way Bakery All-Purpose Flour Mix (purchased or page 211)

1 teaspoon aluminum-free baking powder

1 teaspoon baking soda

½ teaspoon ground cardamom

1 teaspoon Himalayan salt

1 cup fresh, very ripe pears, cored and cut into pieces (peeling is optional)

½ cup maple sugar, coconut sugar, date sugar, or evaporated cane juice

⅓ cup grape seed oil

¼ cup unsweetened applesauce

½ teaspoon ground vanilla bean (or 1 teaspoon gluten-free vanilla extract)

¾ cup full-fat canned coconut milk (or nondairy milk of choice)

Juice of ½ orange

¼ cup Homemade Powdered Sugar (recipe follows)

Pinch of ground or freshly grated nutmeg

Sliced pear, for garnish (optional)

Preheat the oven 350°F. Grease a standard Bundt pan with the palm shortening.

Combine all the dry ingredients (through salt) in a small bowl. Break up any lumps with a whisk.

⟶ recipe continues

Cardamom-Pear Cake with
Orange Glaze,
continued

In a separate bowl, mash the pears (keeping the juice in the bowl) and add the sugar, oil, applesauce, and vanilla. Mix with a hand mixer on medium speed or transfer to a stand mixer with the whisk attachment and mix until just combined. A little at a time, add the dry ingredients to the wet, alternating with the coconut milk and ending with the dry mix. Continue mixing until thoroughly combined.

Pour the batter into the pan and bake for 30 to 40 minutes, checking frequently after 30 minutes. A toothpick should come out clean when inserted into the center. Let cool.

To make the glaze, combine the orange juice and powdered sugar in a small bowl and whisk together until smooth. Drizzle over the cooled cake, garnish with nutmeg and sliced pear if you like, and enjoy!

NORMALLY I don't use *any* cane sugar, but in this recipe, organic evaporated cane juice works better than any other kind of sugar to make a light fluffy powdered sugar you can use for icing and frosting. Make a batch and keep it in an airtight container in the refrigerator. It will last for months.

Makes about 3 cups

2 cups organic evaporated cane juice

1 cup tapioca starch

homemade powdered sugar

Mix the sugar and starch together in a food processor, pulsing until you have a fine powder.

I MADE THIS CAKE for a wedding, and guests said it was the best food there. The idea for the unusual combination of flavors came to my mind one evening when I was sharing an amazing bottle of Brunello Italian wine with friends, along with some figs and chocolate. The flavor of the three together was incredible and I thought, "Well, that should be a cake!" I had never tried to add wine to a dessert before, but why not? The cake is rich and decadent without being too heavy, and the vegan buttercream gives it an extra lightness that transforms the dessert into something other-worldly. Nobody would ever guess it is gluten free and vegan.

Makes one 6-inch cake

Chocolate Cake with Red Wine–Soaked Figs and Vegan Buttercream

5 fresh figs

½ cup good red wine

1 tablespoon palm shortening, nondairy butter (such as Earth Balance), or coconut oil, for greasing the pans

2½ cups Jennifer's Way Bakery All-Purpose Flour (purchased or page 211)

1½ cups organic unsweetened cocoa powder

2½ teaspoons baking soda

2 teaspoons aluminum-free baking powder

1 teaspoon ground vanilla bean (or 2 teaspoons gluten-free vanilla extract)

Pinch of espresso powder

2 teaspoons Himalayan salt

1 very ripe banana

1 cup unsweetened applesauce

1½ cups rice milk, coconut milk, or any other additive-free, unsweetened nondairy milk

1 cup maple sugar, coconut sugar, date sugar, or evaporated cane juice

1 cup real maple syrup

⅔ cup olive oil

⅓ cup warm water

¼ cup melted chocolate (melt any nondairy naturally sweetened chocolate you like in the microwave, stirring after every 15 seconds so it doesn't burn)

Vegan Buttercream (recipe follows)

TO DECORATE

3 tablespoons dairy-free, naturally sweetened chocolate chips

1 tablespoon nondairy butter (such as Earth Balance) or palm shortening

2 or 3 whole fresh figs

Note: This is a very small cake, baked in a 6-inch pan. The good thing about a very small cake is that you can't really overeat it.

The night before, soak the figs in the red wine in the refrigerator. Be sure they soak for at least 5 hours, or up to 12. Before making the cake, drain the figs and cut them into ½-inch slices. Discard any remaining wine.

Preheat the oven to 350°F. Grease two 6-inch cake pans pan with the shortening.

⟶ recipe continues

Chocolate Cake with
Red Wine–Soaked Figs and
Vegan Buttercream,
continued

↳———→

In a medium bowl, combine the flour, cocoa, baking soda, baking powder, vanilla, espresso, and salt and whisk out any lumps.

In a stand mixer with a whisk attachment, combine the banana, applesauce, milk, sugar, maple syrup, and olive oil. Slowly add the dry ingredients to the wet, mixing on low speed as you go. Add the warm water and mix until everything is thoroughly combined. Add the melted chocolate and mix again. Fold in the sliced drained figs.

Pour the batter into the pans, dividing it evenly, and bake for 35 to 45 minutes, until a toothpick inserted in the center comes out clean. Let cool completely.

Once totally cool, put one layer on a plate and cover with buttercream. Top with the second layer and frost the top and sides.

To decorate with chocolate-covered figs, melt the chocolate chips and butter in a bowl in the microwave, stirring after every 15 seconds until smooth. Dip the whole figs in the chocolate, fully or halfway, and put them on parchment paper to cool and harden. Place them on top of the cake.

USE TO FROST the Chocolate Cake with Red Wine–Soaked Figs here or the Carrot Cake on page 289. You can also double the recipe to frost any larger cake, and it's good on cupcakes.

↳——→ *vegan
buttercream*

Makes about 1¹/₂ cups buttercream

1 cup palm shortening

¾ cup Homemade Powdered Sugar (page 282)

2 tablespoons rice milk, coconut milk, or any other additive-free, unsweetened nondairy milk

½ teaspoon ground vanilla bean (or 1 teaspoon gluten-free vanilla extract)

Combine all the ingredients in a bowl and mix with a hand mixer on high speed until fluffy (you could also do this in a stand mixer). The buttercream will keep in an airtight container in the refrigerator for up to 2 weeks.

THIS IS one of our most beloved cakes at my bakery. It's simple but perfect: a light, fresh version of strawberry shortcake that practically screams spring and summer. The cake is best when fresh strawberries are at their peak, bright and bursting with flavor, in late spring.

The recipe uses smaller 6-inch cake pans, which are great to have on hand if you're a baker, but you could also use two 8-inch pans. The layers will be slightly thinner, but it won't make that much difference.

This frosting uses coconut cream. Don't use cream of coconut, which is a processed, highly sweetened product. Coconut cream is the solid cream on top of a chilled can of full-fat coconut milk. That's the good stuff. Chill the cans upside-down the night before. Turn right-side up, open the top, and the cream will be right there, for easy scooping.

Serves 8

Fresh Strawberry Cake with Coconut Cream Frosting

CAKE

1 tablespoon palm shortening, nondairy butter (such as Earth Balance), or coconut oil, for the pans

2 cups Jennifer's Way Bakery All-Purpose Flour Mix (purchased or page 211), plus more for the pans

1 teaspoon aluminum-free baking powder

1 teaspoon baking soda

1 teaspoon Himalayan salt

1 cup unsweetened applesauce

¾ cup maple sugar, coconut sugar, date sugar, or evaporated cane juice

⅓ cup olive oil

1 tablespoon grated lemon zest

¼ cup fresh lemon juice

¾ cup full-fat canned coconut milk (or other nondairy milk of choice)

FROSTING

2 cups Homemade Powdered Sugar (page 282)

1 cup palm shortening or nondairy butter (such as Earth Balance)

2 tablespoons coconut cream (see headnote)

½ teaspoon ground vanilla bean (or 1 teaspoon gluten-free vanilla extract)

2 to 3 cups sliced fresh strawberries

FOR THE CAKE: Preheat the oven to 350°F. Grease two 6-inch round cake pans with the shortening, then lightly flour with flour mix.

Combine all the dry ingredients (through salt) in a small bowl. Break up any lumps with a whisk.

—→ recipe continues

In a stand mixer with a whisk attachment, combine the applesauce, sugar, olive oil, and lemon zest and juice. Mix on low speed until just combined. A little at a time, add the dry ingredients to the wet, alternating with the coconut milk and ending with the dry mix. Continue mixing until thoroughly combined.

Divide the batter between the pans. Bake for 30 to 40 minutes, checking frequently after 30 minutes. A toothpick inserted into the center should come out clean. Let cool, then transfer the cakes to cooling racks.

FOR THE FROSTING: Combine all the ingredients in a medium bowl and whip on high speed with a hand mixer (or use a stand mixer with a whisk attachment) until light and fluffy, about 5 minutes.

To assemble the cake, cut each layer in half horizontally to make 4 thin layers. (If you used 8-inch pans and the layers look too thin to cut, just make the cake with two layers instead of four.) Place one layer on a flat plate or cake stand and gently cover with a generous dollop of frosting. Arrange cut-up strawberries on top of the frosting. Place the next layer of cake on top of the strawberries and repeat the frosting and strawberry steps until you've used up all the cake layers. Finish the cake off with frosting and arrange fresh strawberries on top to decorate.

THIS CAKE REPRESENTS the very first culinary step into my new life. I had taken a day class in gluten-free baking and thought, what the heck, I'm going to give it a shot and bake a cake. Well, four hours later, history was made alongside a warm carrot cake. It took me three years to really perfect the recipe, but that first cake was the seed for Jennifer's Way Bakery. That carrot cake changed my life. I hope it helps change your life too.

Makes two 6-inch cakes or 12 cupcakes

Carrot Cake

Note: There is a grain-free Clean version of this recipe on page 206. Both are nice. You might like to try them both for comparison.

1 tablespoon palm shortening, nondairy butter (such as Earth Balance), or coconut oil, for the pan

2 cups Jennifer's Way Bakery All-Purpose Flour Mix (purchased or page 211)

2 tablespoons aluminum-free baking powder

2 teaspoons baking soda

1 cup maple sugar, coconut sugar, date sugar, or organic evaporated cane juice

2 teaspoons ground cinnamon

1/2 teaspoon ground or freshly grated nutmeg

Pinch of ground cloves

1 teaspoon Himalayan salt

1 ripe banana, mashed

1/2 cup olive oil

1/3 cup real maple syrup

1/4 cup unsweetened applesauce

1 teaspoon ground vanilla bean (or 2 teaspoons gluten-free vanilla extract)

2 cups shredded carrots

3/4 cup walnuts or pecans (optional)

1 recipe Vegan Buttercream (page 285; optional)

Preheat the oven 350°F. Grease two 6-inch cake pans with the shortening, or line a standard 12-cup muffin pan with baking liners.

Combine all the dry ingredients (through salt) in a small bowl. Using a stand mixer with a whisk attachment, combine the banana, olive oil, maple syrup, applesauce, and vanilla and mix on high speed until smooth. Slowly add the dry mixture to the wet. Whisk at medium speed until thoroughly incorporated. Fold in the shredded carrots and nuts, if using them.

Scoop the batter into the cake pan or liners and bake for 25 to 35 minutes for cake (15 to 20 minutes for cupcakes). Avoid opening the oven multiple times to prevent the cake from sinking in the middle—it is delicate. The cake or cupcakes are done when a toothpick inserted into the center comes out clean. Cool completely, then layer the cakes, filling and frosting with buttercream if desired, or frost the cupcakes. These are also delicious without frosting—your call.

Final Thoughts

For now, this is where I leave you. But I hope this cookbook will be a jumping-off point for you as you continue to heal and nourish yourself and learn your way around the kitchen. The more comfortable you get with cooking your own real food with safe, clean ingredients, the better you will get at improvising and even inventing your own recipes. Food can be an endless source of creativity and joy. Food can also be life—a healthy life. You truly are what you eat, and if what you eat is healthy and delicious because it is made in a better way, you will feel the difference. I hope this proves to you that you really can look at food differently. So, get in the kitchen! Your life depends on it. I can't wait to hear your thoughts.

Happy eating!

Acknowledgments

So many have come to see me at my bakery, written me letters, and contacted me on social media, simply to tell me their stories. All I am is somebody out there who *gets it*. If your story is unheard, *I get that*. If you are sick and tired of being sick and tired every day of your life, *I get that*.

More people are beginning to get it too. Even doctors. I would like to thank the doctors out there who understand and know that food is *also* medicine: To the naturopaths, the functional medicine docs, the holistic healers, and also to the clean-food chefs and activists producing and advocating for quality food, thank you for spreading the message. Also, thank you to the health food bloggers and the community who strive to bring us, the public, better quality food and information, so we can all eat cleaner and feel well. They understand that life doesn't have to involve compromises in eating or excuses for health issues. It can be lived fully—happily and deliciously.

I also must thank the warriors who picked me up and carried me when I hit the ground. I treasure you more than words can explain. Deb, Scott, Jesper, Rick, Patrick, Ralph—no words but thank you. Also thanks to Ana, my dear, loyal, enthusiastic, creative, patient, hardworking friend. If it wasn't for you, helping me keep my little 400-square-foot bakery moving, this journey might have ended.

Sometimes hard lessons disguised as people and situations can make you question it all. As painful as some life lessons or health situations are, sometimes the only way to go forward and to grow is by stepping back and allowing the world to simply unfold, to show you what is, rather than only what you wish was true. This is how we move forward—by having gratitude for how we learn and grow, especially when confronted by adversity. We really have only one true choice: always and ever onward!

Index

Note: *Italic page numbers refer to photographs.*

About the Author

Jennifer Esposito is an award-winning actress who has appeared in more than fifteen films and in dozens of TV shows, but she is first and foremost a health advocate. After a diagnosis of celiac disease in 2008, she created and opened Jennifer's Way Bakery in 2013, the first gluten-free, vegan, soy-free, refined-sugar-free, grain-free, and allergy-friendly bakery in Manhattan. Jennifer's Way Bakery now ships to customers across the United States. She is also extremely proud of her *New York Times* bestselling book, *Jennifer's Way*, and she has a blog dedicated to clean living called LivingFreeJennifer.com.